CREDO

Unitarians and Universalists of
Yesteryear Talk About Their
Lives and Motivations

Don McEvoy

CREDO
Copyright © by Donald W. McEvoy 2001

Third Printing

This book is available in quantity
at special discounts for your group or organization.

For information contact:
Don McEvoy
703 Stratford Ct, #11
Del Mar, CA 92014
donmitzimac@aol.com

ISBN 0-9705499-0-3

Printed in the United States of America

This Book is Dedicated
to
Carolyn, Tom, Liz, Paige and all
the other freethinking mystics
with helping hands.

FOREWORD

A feature of many Sunday mornings at First Unitarian-Universalist Church in San Diego is the presentation of a Credo by some member or friend of the congregation.

The Credo is an alpine moment for me. I am always inspired, frequently astonished, and often amused by these open, honest, revealing, probing statements of personal faith and the biographical guideposts which describe the odyssey which led the speaker to that place.

Another thing, which has piqued my interest since joining this particular band of pilgrims, is the number of prominent Americans of the past who were either Unitarian or Universalist. It is truly astonishing.

Wouldn't it be interesting, I thought, to hear their Credos? But, alack and alas, they are all long since dead. That sent me back to the library, to study the biographies, diaries, essays and speeches. What I found is what you will find on the following pages. Whenever practical I have used the exact words of the person speaking.

In my research I discovered that several persons whom Unitarians claim as their own were never actually affiliated. But I have involved them, too. They were certainly friends of this movement in significant ways.

Some may find these pages useful in congregational worship or religious education activities. For others they may be an introduction to a liberal and liberating religious movement of which they had little or no knowledge. Or they may simply provide others with the opportunity for enlightening and inspirational conversations with thirty-seven quite remarkable persons from our past.

Whatever your quest, I hope you enjoy the journey.

SPEAKERS

Good morning, I am
Thomas Jefferson

I have been asked to offer a brief statement of my personal religious beliefs on this occasion.

I found this a strange request. Anyone who knows me should know that I have frequently stated "I inquire after no man's religious opinions, and trouble none with mine." I have never regarded matters of religious faith a proper subject for public debate. Nonetheless, in this particular venue, I shall attempt to accede to your request.

I suppose the place to start would be with words with which you are quite familiar:

• I believe that all men are created equal and are endowed by their Creator with certain unalienable rights, among which are life, liberty, and the pursuit of happiness.

• I believe every person should be free to speak as he chooses.

• I believe in the importance of a free press, even if it does not live up to my standards of responsibility.

• I believe that society probably needs a revolution every twenty-five years or so to assure that government does not grow so strong as to stifle the liberties of the individual citizens.

And, as you will remember, I pledged my "undying enmity to every form of tyranny over the mind of man."

There is the core of my beliefs. I wish it were also the reality of my actions. Unfortunately that is not so. There were a number of irreconcilable contradictions in my life. The central one, I am sure, is that while declaring the equality of all men, and speaking

1

often of the evil of the slave trade, I owned slaves throughout my life. I can only say now that I was a product of my times. Even though I seemed to be ahead of my times in many ways, it was not so in all things.

Also, if any of you came today hoping to hear some titillating inside information about my relationship with Sally Hemmings, you will leave disappointed. I consider that a deeply personal matter and out of the bounds of public discourse.

As I review my very active and interesting life, three accomplishments stand out. They are the ones I decreed should be etched on my gravestone: Authorship of the Declaration of Independence, passage of the Virginia Statute of Religious Freedom, and the founding and developing of the University of Virginia.

In my first term as a member of the House of Burgesses, in 1769 when I was only twenty-four years of age, I offered the Religious Freedom Statute for consideration. Since the Commonwealth had been established in Jamestown in 1607, the Church of England held privileges denied to all others. My proposal called for complete disestablishment and the erection of a wall of separation between Church and State. There were some in our legislative body who were willing to go part of the way by granting tolerance for dissenting groups, but I refused any halfway measures. I said at the time, "We must comprehend within the mantle of its protection the Jew, the Gentile, the Christian, the Mahomentan, the Hindoo, and the infidel of every denomination."

It took me ten long and arduous years, but in1779 when I was serving as Governor, the Virginia Statute for Religious Freedom was finally enacted. Not many years later these principles were incorporated into the American Bill of Rights. It will come as no surprise to you that my espousal of religious liberty resulted in my being branded an anarchist, an atheist, an infidel, even the anti-Christ.

During my first campaign for the presidency, clergymen in New England urged their congregants to hide their Bibles because "Jefferson plans to confiscate them if he is elected."

2

I am told that one Methodist minister, when baptizing a child, asked the child's name. When the father replied, Thomas Jefferson, the preacher said: "That is no name for a Christian. I baptize you John Adams". Surely he was unaware that John Adams was a Boston Unitarian!

I chose not to respond to any of these deprecations and insinuations. As I said before, I never regarded matters of religious belief a proper subject for public debate.

Through friendships with John Adams, John Russell and Benjamin Rush I became acquainted with the thinking of both the Unitarians and the Universalists, and was later deeply influenced by the British Unitarian preacher and scientist Joseph Priestly.

I never joined a Unitarian Church. There were none in Virginia to join. But, as I wrote to a friend, "I must content myself with being a Unitarian by myself, assured that many around me would do the same if they could only hear the matter fairly stated."

Good morning, I am
Abigail Adams

I arrived on this earth in mid-November of the year 1744, the daughter of Reverend William Smith and his wife Dorothy of Weymouth, Massachusetts.

My father, Parson Smith was not a great man as the world judges, but he was a man of character, intelligence and cultivation. My mother was the daughter of Colonel John Quincy of Boston.

The winter of that year was a time of epidemic of what we may suppose to have been diphtheria, or some kindred affliction. I was one of very few infants born that winter who survived to a first birthday.

I was never sent to any school. It was, in fact, fashionable to ridicule female learning in those days. But formal schooling was not necessary for me. There were books aplenty in my father's study and at the home of my grandfather Quincy, where I spent a considerable amount of time. I have never forgotten the excellent lessons I received from my grandmother at a very early period in my life.

Grandmother Quincy and I corresponded regularly during my childhood. I am forever grateful that she formed my letter writing habit early. My husband, John, and I were separated so much of our married life that I only survived through the writing of letters.

I met John through the acquaintance of John Hancock, whose family lived nearby. Hancock was seven years older than I, but we had seen each other often and been friends throughout our childhoods.

John Adams, son of a farmer in Braintree, was a Harvard classmate of John Hancock and after graduation a frequent visitor to our town. John Adams engaged himself in the study of law, and in 1758, after his admission to the Massachusetts bar, came knocking on the door of Parson Smith asking the hand of his daughter Abigail in marriage.

The Family at Large was mightily disturbed. Law was a new profession, probably a dangerous and iniquitous one. The Quincys all shook their heads emphatically. What! Abigail with her wit, beauty, gentle blood and breeding, marry "one of that dishonest tribe of lawyers," the son of a small country farmer? Perish the thought!

All but my father, who approved of the match! On our wedding day he conveyed a reproach to the family and parishioners by preaching a sermon from Luke 7:33. "For John came neither eating bread nor drinking wine, and ye say, 'He hath a devil.'"

The first ten years of our married life were spent in Braintree where John practiced law and I produced four children, one daughter and three sons. But circumstances about us demanded changes. The Boston Massacre, the Tea Party, John's election to the Continental Congress, the Declaration of Independence. All required his attention, and enforced separation from his family.

On the last day of March 1776 I wrote him in Philadelphia. You probably know of that letter. I urged the members of the Continental Congress to "remember the ladies and be more generous and favorable to them than your ancestors."

"Do not put such unlimited power into the hands of the husbands. Remember, all men would be tyrants if they could."

"If particular care and attention is not paid to the ladies, we are determined to foment a rebellion, and will not hold ourselves bound by any laws in which we have no voice or representation."

I was not at all pleased by John's reply, which treated my words lightly. "We have been told," he wrote "that our struggle has loosened the bonds of government everywhere; that children and apprentices were disobedient; that schools and colleges were grown turbulent; that Indians slighted their guardians, and Negroes grew insolent to their masters. But your letter was the first intimation that another tribe, more numerous and more powerful than all the rest, were grown discontented."

I could not let the matter drop at that. I responded: "Whilst you are proclaiming peace and goodwill to men, emancipating all nations, you insist on retaining an absolute power over wives. But you must remember that arbitrary power is, like most other things which are very hard, very liable to be broken and notwithstanding all your wise laws and maxims, we have it in our power, not only to free ourselves, but to subdue our masters, and, and without violence, throw both voluntary and legal authority at our feet."

Such differences, you must understand, never strained our love for one another. Through every kind of vexation and enforced separation we remained committed to one another throughout our lives.

Lives which took us to Europe where John was ambassador to the Court of St. James, to Philadelphia where he served as our nation's first Vice President under President George Washington, to Washington where we were the first occupants of the White House while John served as America's second President. And finally to Massachusetts for retirement after he was defeated for reelection by his old friend Thomas Jefferson.

John and I were both of Puritan stock and rearing, but each of us individually, and the two of us together, evolved over the years a much more liberal and universal religious view. I can't recall exactly when, but we began to identify ourselves to any who inquired as adherents of a Unitarian belief. I'm sure our lives of public service were stimulated by that faith.

Good morning. I am
Dr. Benjamin Rush

I come from a long line of dissenters. Among my ancestors were John and Susanna Rush who arrived in Pennsylvania in 1683, just one year after William Penn had established his colony. They settled on the banks of the Delaware River, twelve miles north of Philadelphia.

Five generation later, in 1746, I was born to John and Susanna Rush. My father died when I was only five years of age, and at nine I was sent to Maryland to live and study with an uncle, the Reverend Dr. Samuel Finley. In addition to my training in the classics, I was schooled in the stern Presbyterianism of my foster parent.

At thirteen I was enrolled in the College of New Jersey, which 150 years later was renamed Princeton University. After two years there I was granted a Bachelor's degree.

It was expected that I would enter an apprenticeship for the study of law, but I was not yet ready, at fifteen, to make that decision. I vacillated between an interest in becoming a minister, or maybe a lawyer, or maybe a physician. After only a few months I placed myself under the tutelage of Dr. John Redman of Philadelphia to prepare myself for a life in medicine. I completed my medical education in two years at the University of Edinburgh.

The years abroad introduced me to the ideas of the Enlightenment, which I was able to adapt to my theological mentality. I also became a member of Edinburgh's Revolution Club, which was good training for what I would face upon my return to Philadelphia.

I came home to practice medicine, and burning with a new appreciation for the rights of man with an acute sense of the inequities of our society, and determined that the colonies of the New World must demand freedom from the Old.

My religious views had been altered also. I lost none of the fervor I had gained from the Great Awakening, but had become much more inclusive in my thinking, as I moved from concepts of judgment to a belief in Universal salvation at the hands of an all-loving God.

As was not unusual among the educated classes of those days, I wrote frequent short articles proposing independence that were published in local newspapers. But, in the fall of 1775, I conceived the idea of a longer pamphlet addressed to the American people on the necessity of separation from Great Britain.

After having prepared most of the text for such a publication I began to worry about a possible negative effect on my growing medical practice if I published as I planned.

A young friend, recently arrived from England, had no such inhibitions. He took what I had already written, added other ideas of his own, and skillfully edited the whole. Then, in early January 1776, Thomas Paine published Common Sense.

His words burst from the press with an effect rarely produced by any paper in any age or locale.

Six months later I had the privilege of adding my signature to the Declaration of Independence, written by my young friend from Virginia, Thomas Jefferson.

For others this may have been only a political act. To me it represented an opportunity for the establishment of the Kingdom of God on earth. The American Revolution was, for me, the vital preliminary to a new civilization in which true Christianity would flourish among free men. It would be the establishment of a Christian utopia where, in a paradise regained, the forces of reason and revelation would triumph over all physical and moral evil.

A few years later when the Constitution of the new Republic was being debated, I proposed that a Congress of representatives from each Christian sect be established as an ecclesiastical federal

8

government to promote national morality. Like the political states in the new federal union, the sects would be protected by a constitution of their sovereign rights.

I believed that by such a system the decadent ways of European society might be replaced by rational settlements of differences, brotherly love and peace and benevolence to all mankind. I saw a new world of virtuous citizens living harmoniously in the world's first truly Christian Republic.

I thought we could abolish slavery, outlaw cruel public and capital punishments, dueling, war and other sundry institutions and practices which detracted from human worth and dignity.

As I told the American Philosophical Society in 1786, I am not so sanguine as to suppose that it is possible for man to acquire so much perfection from science, religion, liberty and good government, as to cease to be mortal; but I am fully persuaded, that from the combined action of causes, which operate upon the reason, the passions, the senses, the brain, the nerves, the blood, the heart, it is possible to produce such a change in his moral character, as shall raise him to a semblance of angels; nay, more, to the likeness of God Himself.

As I told people 200 years ago, I say to you: The American Revolution is not over yet!

Good morning. I am
William Ellery Channing

When I was a young boy, probably eight or nine, I'm not exactly sure, my father took me with him to see a famous evangelist who was preaching at a revival meeting near our home in Newport, Rhode Island.

The preacher spoke loud and long and he made it quite clear that God was angry with the world, and that the people in it were all sinners, and except for a very few the worst was yet to come. Most were doomed to everlasting torture and death.

Father shook hands with the preacher when the service was over. I heard him say, "Very good sermon, sir. Sound doctrine!" Then on the way home he seemed in a very cheerful mood. He whistled as the carriage went along. And when we got home, he joined the family in a hearty Sunday dinner and settled down to read the Sunday paper.

"How was this possible," I wondered. How could he be so happy and comfortable when such a terrible fate awaited most of the human race, including, probably, some members of his own family?

I never did resolve that question, but I did spend considerably more time observing our neighbors, friends and others whom I met along the way. They may have had some minor flaws, I thought, but to me they seemed basically good. I didn't go around Newport saying it aloud, but I decided at a very early age that the Calvinists were wrong – and that my father probably knew it too, but just didn't want to raise a fuss.

I was born in 1780, while the Revolutionary War was being fought. My father was a lawyer. Mother was the daughter of William Ellery who was a signer of the Declaration of Independence and later a member of Congress. It was simply assumed that I would attend Harvard and make a career in law. Father died suddenly the year before I was scheduled to enter Harvard, but he left sufficient resources for me to pursue my studies. Four years later, when it was time to graduate, I found that I did not want to be a lawyer, but I wished to become a minister.

I took off a year and hired out as a tutor for a family in Richmond, Virginia to save up enough money to continue on to the Harvard Divinity School. I discovered much about the Southern way of life that appealed to me, but was repulsed by seeing, first hand and for the first time, the institution of slavery. Aristocratic society, with all of its values, was built on the ownership of slaves. This I could not bear.

I went back to Harvard, completed my ministerial studies, was ordained in the Congregational Church and assumed the pastorate of Federal Street Church in Boston. You will probably be surprised to hear that I was a relatively orthodox minister in those early years.

There was quite a bit of ferment in the churches during the aftermath of the Revolution. One new church established in Pennsylvania was named "Unitarian". A number of the clergy of the liberal wing of the New England Congregationalists were preaching Unitarian views about the nature of God and the role of Jesus, as well as the more important questions about the right of persons to think for themselves. But I took little notice of these controversies. I was far more interested in people than I was in theology and simply had no stomach for controversy and debate.

Reversing the usual pattern of starting out liberal and gradually becoming more conservative with age, I seemed to grow more liberal (radical, if you wish) as time went by. Someone said about me that I was "always young for freedom." I like that. I like that very much!

When a group of more conservative Congregational clergy, growing impatient over the number of ministers preaching

Unitarian ideas, demanded a showdown – calling on "all true Christians to separate themselves" from those with Unitarian leanings, I tried to interpose myself as a mediator and a peacemaker. I refused to take sides with either faction.

But, five years later, as the controversy grew more bitter and rancorous, I took advantage of an invitation to preach an ordination sermon for a young man in the Unitarian Church in Baltimore, Maryland. I "came out" if you please, calling the Calvinist doctrine of "election" an "insult to both God and man." I pleaded for a church that would teach what Jesus taught about the need to love God and love our fellow men. Much to my surprise this Baltimore Sermon became the rallying point and marked the beginning of an organizational relationship of Unitarian Churches. Within quite a short period of time more than 125 congregations had voted to become Unitarian. In 1825 the American Unitarian Association was formed and a new denomination was created. This had not been my intention at all but it was how things turned out.

I was also slow in coming to terms with the struggle to free the slaves. I hated slavery. It was an abomination. But I had little in common with the militant abolitionists and held myself at arms length from them for far too long. It was not until I was chided by a young friend whose opinion I held in highest regard, that I acknowledged the justice of his reproof, and admitted I had been silent for too long. From that day on I worked diligently for abolition.

I had a good and productive life, though a far from predictable one. I had great distaste for controversy, yet I was involved in the most controversial issues of my day. I was also reluctant, even timid, to fostering social change, yet I became hailed as a great reformer. I tried to distance myself from sectarian concerns, yet became the father of a new denomination.

Follow your conscience, my friends. Your inner light. You never know where it will lead you.

Good morning. I am
Horace Mann

Universal free public education was one of the dreams of the founders of this nation. Yet, it took the better part of the century to bring that dream to reality.

Forty years had already elapsed since George Washington was inaugurated as the president of the new nation before I led the state of Massachusetts in establishing a comprehensive and functional program for free public education. And, we were the first state to accomplish this.

There was little in my background to predict that I would grow up to become the "father of the public schools." I was not a professional educator. Our family had been farmers for five generations. Until I was fifteen years old I never attended school more than eight or ten weeks a year.

Through a stroke of good fortune I received a bequest making it possible for me to study at Brown University in Providence, Rhode Island.

I made the best of that opportunity, studied law, developed a successful practice in Boston, entered politics and was elected to the state Senate.

During these years in Boston I became acquainted with Ellery Channing, the Unitarian minister at Federal Street Church. Through a friendship with Elizabeth Peabody, whose younger sister Mary I later married, I met Emerson and the others in his Transcendentalist group. Early in my teens I had broken with the stern Calvinism of my childhood, and discovered in Unitarianism a liberal spirit with which I was comfortable.

I was not always comfortable, however with many in Channing's congregation. I found them too rich and exclusive for my tastes. I frequently walked down to the waterfront to hear the preaching of Jeremy Taylor at the Seaman's Bethel. On the outside Channing and Taylor could not have been more different, but I found in each a message of universal atonement and humanitarian concern for social reforms.

When in 1837, my forty-first year, the Massachusetts State Senate wrestled with the problem of public education, I became the most outspoken advocate for reform. Consequently, when it was decided to appoint a State Board to oversee the matter, I was designated as its head. My salary in this new post was $1,500, about half what I was earning as an attorney. But I said, to myself and to the public, "the interests of a client are small compared to the interests of the next generation. So, let the next generation be my client."

For the next four years I labored for that client. Everyday was a skirmish, and major battles were not infrequent. The first struggle was against a coalition of local political officials who were fearful that a statewide effort would weaken their power. Then came the battles to open more teaching positions to women, to establish criteria for standards of teaching, to include music and art in the curriculum along with reading and writing and arithmetic, to develop libraries for the schools, to raise the salaries of teachers.

The biggest battle, of course, was to maintain the secular nature and religious neutrality of the public schools. Evangelicals and the American Sunday School Union were unrelenting in their efforts to get sectarian Christian materials into the curriculum of almost every academic subject.

My resistance to their efforts led, of course, to accusations that I was anti-Christian, an advocate of atheism, and a zealot in efforts to open the doors of the common schools to Godless secularism. In Massachusetts we won that battle for a period of time. But I suspect it is never really finished. It probably has to be fought anew in every generation.

Following my twelve years of labor in that vineyard, I ran for public office again. I succeeded John Quincy Adams in the U.S. House of Representatives and served two terms.

Then I made the mistake of allowing Samuel Gridley Howe and the radical Unitarian minister Theodore Parker to talk me into running for Governor as the Free Soil candidate.

On Election Day only 27% of the voters supported me. I was the anti-slavery and temperance candidate. The supporters of slavery and rum were victorious.

The next day I accepted the presidency of a new college, Antioch, which was being established in Yellow Springs, Ohio. A small relatively liberal denomination, called the Christian Connexion had decided to create the school.

Their original intent was to build it in New England, but some wealthy land speculators in the west convinced them to build in Ohio, believing that the presence of a college would bring about a population boom to the area.

Yellow Springs was selected as the site for the new metropolis they were sure would emerge.

They were committed to excellence in scholarship and the adoption of many of the progressive educational theories I held dear. We started well but within five years the boom turned to bust. The speculators reneged on their pledges. There were no resources to continue. That is when the Unitarians stepped forward and permitted Antioch to survive. I spent the rest of my life on that campus.

My Credo is probably in an admonition I offered at my final Baccalaureate address: Be ashamed to die until you have won some victory for humanity!

Good morning. I am
Samuel Gridley Howe

I was a physician, a social reformer, a journalist, a teacher, an abolitionist, a statesman, and a philanthropist. But I am probably best remembered as the husband of remarkable Julia Ward Howe.

I was born in Boston in 1801 to a family whose roots ran deep in Massachusetts. My grandfather was one of the "Indians" at the Boston Tea Party, and my great uncle was the engineer who designed the Patriot fortifications on Bunker Hill.

The Howes were Jeffersonian Republicans in an overwhelmingly Federalist city, and I learned early what it meant to be a non-conformist. But I must have been drawn to that condition, selecting Brown University over Harvard for my college education. As a Unitarian I would have fit in easily at Harvard, and represented quite a challenge to the Baptists at Brown.

It was there I met Horace Mann who became a lifelong friend and my colleague in many social reforms. Horace, along with the poet Henry Wadsworth Longfellow, the radical minister Theodore Parker and the orator and Senator Charles Sumner – Unitarians every one – were my closest and most cherished associates.

After college I attended Harvard Medical School, graduating in 1824 with little idea of what I wanted to do with the rest of my life. The confluence of an unhappy romance, youthful adventuring and social conscience led me halfway around the world as a volunteer in the Greek War of Independence. I joined as an army surgeon and returned five years later as the Chevalier of the Order of St. Savior. Forever I was known to my wife and closest friends simply as "Chev".

Once back in Massachusetts I was offered the directorship of the New England Asylum for the Blind. I accepted the position and immediately sailed for Europe where I spent a year studying the newest methods for fulfilling such a difficult and demanding position. I continued as head of that institution for nearly fifty years.

Early on I proposed we expand our mission to include those who were deaf as well as those who were blind, but was not able to get official permission. Then Laura Bridgman was brought to me. She became my most famous student. Left both deaf and blind by scarlet fever shortly after her first birthday, she seemed to be doomed to a life of loneliness and a sub-human existence. Using our newly developed and admittedly experimental methods, Laura learned to read and communicate with signs.

It was nearly a century later that Helen Keller mastered similar accomplishments. It was Laura, in fact, who brought Julia and me together. Julia Ward was the daughter of the influential New York banker, Samuel Ward. While visiting in Boston in the summer of 1841 she heard talk about Laura, "the miracle child," and came to the institute to see her. If you have been keeping track you know that I was forty years old at the time and I was a confirmed bachelor. My friends thought I would never marry. They were wrong.

Two years later Julia and I were married, but only after I made it clearly understood I was not interested in her fortune, and even forbade her family paying for our wedding.

The only thing I could not talk her out of was the retention of her maiden name. She claimed the right to be known as Mrs. Julia Ward Howe and not as Mrs. Samuel Gridley Howe, as I wished. As I told her many times throughout our years together, I was a reformer, not a revolutionary, and was not prepared to deal with a "modern woman."

How can I summarize so full a life? I served side by side with my friend Horace Mann in battles to create the Common Schools of Massachusetts.

17

I was closely associated with that little Unitarian powerhouse, Dorothea Dix, in getting the insane out of prisons and into hospitals for treatment instead of punishment.

I dedicated more than twenty years of my life to the struggle to abolish slavery in America. Among my many activities in this regard were leadership in Vigilance Committee to protect fugitive slaves from bounty hunters who operated under the authority of the Fugitive Slave Act. I served as head of the Massachusetts Emigrant Aid Company, which underwrote expenses of those who moved to Kansas to keep that territory from becoming a slave state. I led the campaign to get Charles Sumner elected to the U.S. Senate, where he became the most outspoken opponent of slavery.

I also became a part of a secret group of six who gave money to support John Brown, first in his efforts against the Border Ruffians in Kansas, and later in his ill-fated raid on the U.S. Arsenal at Harpers Ferry. I can honestly say that I did not know, in advance, of his plans to attack the arsenal. Still, in retrospect it seems I should have suspected some daring of that magnitude.

I was involved I suppose, in every philanthropic and social reformation of the 19th century including the women's movement, despite what you might hear on the matter from Julia.

So, social reform is my Credo. The quest for truth is my sacrament, and service is my prayer.

Good morning. I am
Dorothea Dix

I was born in the year 1802 in a hut on an isolated farm near Hampden, Maine. My parents had been sent there by my grandfather, who owned huge tracts of land in the region. He, for some reason, thought they could work out problems in their marriage in that bleak and stark environment.

Rather it drove my father to drink and to religious fanaticism, and my mother to chronic invalidism. Mine was not a happy childhood.

At twelve I ran away to live with an older sister in Worcester, Massachusetts. One of my cousins liked the stories I told and said I would make a good teacher. So, at age fourteen, I opened my own school for younger children.

At eighteen I moved to Boston to live with my grandmother. I also began to attend church with her. It was a Unitarian Church where Dr. William Ellery Channing was the minister. His influence guided me throughout the rest of my life.

The plight of the poor children in Boston caused me great pain. I asked my grandmother for permission to use the hayloft in her carriage house as a school for those impoverished ones. She resisted, but I persisted. At last she said, "Have your school for beggars, then!" So, in addition to my regular teaching position, I opened a second school.

Dr. Channing and his family spent their summers at a home in Rhode Island, overlooking Narragansett Bay. For several years they took me along as governess for their daughters. There is no way I can tell you what an inspiration it was to spend those intimate times with such a family.

After fifteen years of teaching I suffered a nervous and physical collapse. Dr. Channing arranged for me to go to England and be cared for by his friend Dr. William Rathbone. For eighteen months he and his wife nursed me back to health. More than that they adopted me into their circle of friends, which included Samuel Tuke. He was the builder of the Retreat of York, the first modern mental hospital in the world, where mentally ill patients were given books to read and music to enjoy.

He told me of the terrible conditions of the insane in many parts of England, where they were imprisoned in dungeons, chained to posts, thrown food as if they were animals, and often put on display for a fee. I could not believe what I was hearing.

While I was in England my grandmother died, leaving me a legacy, which provided enough for me to live on. I returned to Boston determined to find out if the treatment of the insane differed in my own country.

What I soon discovered was that the deranged, the paupers, and the violent criminals were all thrown together in the same prisons. All were considered demon possessed and perverted and the jailers seemed to think themselves to be instruments to punish these "evildoers."

I took my findings to Dr. Channing, who put me in touch with three of his influential friends: politician Charles Sumner, educator Horace Mann, and physician Dr. Samuel Gridley Howe. I explained to them that the conditions I had found in Boston were probably true throughout all of Massachusetts and that the legislature should take action on the problem.

They responded that someone would have to visit the jails and almshouses of the state and document the true conditions. That, they said, would take considerable time and considerable money. I told them I would undertake that survey myself.

And I did. Eighteen months later Dr. Howe presented my report to the legislature. It documented my findings of horror. A woman in Dedham, who seemed quite sane, chained in a dark stall behind the almshouse. No one could recall how long she had been there or why she was there at all. In Medford, a man kept in a stall for seventeen years. At Shelburne, an old naked man with his feet frozen off, but the stumps in chains. And on and on and on.

Two years later the Massachusetts legislature voted funds to build a new special hospital for the insane at Worcester. That was the first of 123 asylums and hospitals, which were built through my efforts over the next three decades.

I traveled more than thirty thousand miles from Canada to the Gulf of Mexico, from the Atlantic to the Mississippi, observing the treatment of the insane and proposing new and humane methods of care. It was fascinating to observe the gradual change of attitude. Shortly after I began my study of the conditions in New Jersey, a resolution was passed in the legislature providing $1000 "to get Miss Dix across the Delaware River and out of the state." Three years later they appropriated funds to build a hospital, which became a model for the nation.

During the Civil War I was appointed Supervisor of nurses for the Union Army. For four long years, without a single furlough, I pursued that assignment. It was so demanding that I almost lost the self-control, which I had so carefully cultivated over the years.

Then I went back to New Jersey to spend the remainder of my years in a suite they provided for me in that magnificent hospital.

Good morning. I am
George Ripley

Theologians of my day thought me a radical. Conservative politicians thought me a vigorous activist. Transcendentalists considered me an articulate spokesman. A controversial figure, I tried throughout my life to speak and act meaningfully about capitalism, socialism, feminism, racism, education, labor unions.

I was born in 1803 at Greenfield, Massachusetts in the heart of the Berkshires. My father had moved there twenty-five years earlier, established a tavern and a general store and had become the wealthiest man in town. He was a moderate Puritan who used his influence to gerrymander the town to create a new parish more suitable to his tastes in religion.

It was his moderate faith which accompanied me to Harvard in 1820 where I studied for the ministry. That year William Ellery Channing preached his famous Baltimore sermon, which became the birth of the Unitarian movement. Gradually I adopted Unitarianism, finding it clear and logical rather than blind allegiance to a creed.

But even before completing Divinity School I had moved on to a place independent of any branch of theology. My Credo was simply: "Beloved, let us love one another, for God is love; and he that loveth dwelleth in God and God in him." Unitarianism, for me, was not an end in itself. Rather it was a corkscrew for getting to the sacramental wine – far more useful than the hot hammer of Puritanism.

Upon graduating I settled as minister of the Purchase Street

Church, across the street from the site of the Boston Tea Party. The congregation was so uninspiring that a preacher ran the risk of falling into a dead palsy.

My intellectual life and societal engagements were kept alive during these years by my growing involvement with that remarkable group called the Transcendentalists. It was I, in fact, who convened the first meeting of what began simply as a club for intellectual discussion.

After twelve years with the Purchase Street Church, I resigned to pursue a new, and revolutionary, direction. I was convinced that the necessary next step was to create a community in which our Transcendental beliefs could be tested and displayed as a model for a new social order.

I dreamed of creating a community in which labor and learning, farming and philosophy would stand side by side. A place where human potential could bloom into its fullest flower. A society, in fact, which could supplant capitalism and its inequities as the norm for mankind.

I found my utopian site, my new Garden of Eden, the summer after my resignation from the ministry. It was a farm in West Roxbury, only a few miles outside of Boston. Thus members of the community could get into Boston for the cultural events they wished to attend. With a dream, a plan, and now a place, the Brook Farm experiment could begin.

It was, in the beginning, a capitalist venture. Shares were sold for $500, which made participants full partners. A weekly quota of sixty hours constructive contribution was required of all members. These might be divided according to individual ability and inclination, between plowing, cleaning stables, milking the cows, working in the kitchen, playing the violin or writing poetry.

I was disappointed that not more of my Transcendentalist colleagues joined the venture. Emerson, Channing, Margaret Fuller and others gave support but did not participate. Thoreau chose solitude instead. Nathaniel Hawthorn lived with us for one year, but left after discovering, as he put it, that "half a day shoveling manure does not properly inspire me for the half day of writing I wish to accomplish."

Membership was never a problem. We were flooded with applications from those disenchanted with American materialism. We kept the central core at a manageable thirty or so, but more than four thousand others spent limited periods of time with us in a variety of roles.

In a way we were victims of our own success. The pressing need to expand kept us constantly buying more acres to farm. In 1847, our sixth year of operation, we invested most of our working capital in the construction of a new sufficiently spacious living quarter for the community. When construction was nearing completion, a fire destroyed the new building. We were left with no operating funds. Members were forced against their will to leave and seek other means of livelihood. In the fall of that year Brook Farm was sold to pay off our remaining debts.

I was broken hearted but I moved on. I subsequently had a fulfilling career in New York as a writer and literary critic. Despite this later success, many considered me a failure. Perhaps I failed as a Unitarian minister, and Brook Farm did not accomplish its goal; but I never grew bitter and never stopped believing.

What do I believe? I believe in the recognition of the divine in man and nature. I believe in good and true and beautiful men and women as the incarnation of the inconceivable God. When humanity adopts this faith a new millennium will dawn upon the nations, social harmony will be inaugurated, and this "nasty" world will be transfigured into the heavenly Zion.

Good morning. I am
Ralph Waldo Emerson

I was born in the parish house of First Church, Boston where my father was the minister. My lineage included seven Puritan clergymen. From my first breath there was little question what my vocation would be.

Father died when I was eight years old, leaving my widowed mother with nothing more than a family of seven children. In those days people said, "She was left in Providence." Providence in our case was the Reverend Ezra Ripley, who gave us lodging in his parsonage.

My education consisted of Latin School, Harvard, and the ceaseless tutoring of my Aunt Mary. Dear, sweet, eccentric Aunt Mary who introduced me to the study of world religions, particularly Eastern mysticism.

A problem with my eyesight interrupted my studies at Harvard Divinity School. Nonetheless, the Unitarian Ministers' Association granted me a license to preach without being subjected to the usual examination. Because I had not been able to take notes at lectures, they waived the exam. In retrospect I am sure that was a blessing. For even at that early date my religious convictions were so far removed from orthodoxy that I might never have been approved had I been subjected to the usual questioning.

At age twenty-six I became the minister of Boston's Second Unitarian Church. I liked preaching, but detested most of the other ministerial duties. I recall a particular visit to one dying man. After a little while, he said, "Young man, if you don't know your business you might as well just leave." Even my beloved Aunt Mary, who rarely found any fault in me, confessed once, "Waldo is not very good with funerals."

My fundamental problem, however, was that my beliefs were honeycombed with doubts. Week by week I seemed to move further from acceptance of traditional doctrine; further from a personal God, from an authoritative church, from an historic Christ, from an exclusive Scripture, and lived closer to an evangel of a self enlightened soul. After three years I asked the congregation to relieve me of my duty of officiating at Communion. I proposed they do away with the traditional wine and bread, and simply use that time to meditate on the Founder. They refused. I resigned.

Leaving the ministry was no traumatic experience for me. It seemed the proper thing to do. I felt I was leaving an antiquated profession, which had outlived its usefulness. I was free to pack away the Christian dress in which my thoughts had been clothed, and present those ideas in Transcendental attire.

Two decades earlier, under the leadership of the brilliant William Ellery Channing, the Unitarians had moved out of the Congregational Church and become a denomination of their own. Previously they had been simply the liberal wing of the older established church. But even now, they held fast to many of the traditional beliefs of Christian history. I felt it necessary to move far beyond that.

Transcendentalists believed that God was not somewhere outside of man, but an indwelling presence. We believed that knowledge of God was not limited to those who subscribed to any one doctrine or followed the disciplines of any one religious institution.

In 1838 I spoke at the Harvard Divinity School. In that address, among other things, I reversed the traditional teaching of the church about Jesus. The church taught that Jesus had been a divine being who became human for the purpose of revealing the nature of God to man. I said that he was a human who became divine by being sensitive and responsive to the godliness, which was innate within him, as it is in every human being.

It took the Divinity School a generation to recover from the controversy stimulated by that speech.

I was reviled as a heretic, atheist, the anti-Christ. Except for a small radical group of friends within the ranks, even the Unitarians condemned me. But I never responded to these attacks. I never offered rebuttal of any kind. I refused every challenge to debate the issue. I was perfectly confident in my own integrity. Looking back, I think what I offered the world was confirmation and validation of those mystical moments that visit the soul. Everyone has known such moments when they are in the presence of an unknown element in human destiny, and are subject to a feeling of which they can make no analysis, and whose meaning they cannot read. These are the stirrings of our divine nature, the gift of every person, of every caste and clime.

My hope is that, as the years have gone by, I have become something of a priest to those who have left the church, who found the institution static and arid, but who retain some emotional religious life, some fragment of the ancient heavens, some appreciation of the feeling of the divine.

Good morning. I am
Elizabeth Palmer Peabody

I am so pleased to be with you today to share my personal statement of belief and commitment.

My heart was filled a few minutes ago when those beautiful children led this congregation in their Affirmation. Why, it was my affirmation, too. Exactly!

A mind that is open to the eternal search for truth, with certainty that the search will never be completely successful!

A heart that is open and compassionate not only to those who to us are lovable, but to every member of the entire human family!

Hands which are outstretched to welcome the stranger, and which are busy in the service of others!

God bless the children! They have presented my Credo for me.

The only part of my Credo, which they left out, was what I heard from my mother throughout my growing up years. "You are a genius, Elizabeth," she told me again and again. "You are creative, brilliant, strong, wise and lovely to behold." She said it so often I came to believe it. What a wonderful legacy for a parent to leave with a child.

I spent my life trying to live up to that. I was born in Billerica, Massachusetts in 1804. I grew up to become a teacher, and a close friend of Nathaniel Hawthorne, Ralph Waldo Emerson and William Ellery Channing. All of whom were prominent, progressive leaders of the Unitarian movement.

In fact, I served Reverend Channing for several years as his private secretary, researcher, and copyist for his sermons. So, those stirring words and lofty ideas, which led to the formation of the American Unitarian Association, were reviewed by me even before they were publicly spoken.

I also worked with Bronson Alcott, Louisa May's father, in his experimental Temple School. My publication, *The Record of a School*, was written to make his ideas more widely known. That apparently succeeded so well that shortly after its publication we were both branded as dangerous radicals and the school was forced to close.

I then opened a bookstore in Boston, which became a central meeting place for Emerson and the other members of the Transcendentalist club, as well as other social reformers.

Margaret Fuller's conversations for women began in my bookstore. These sessions were, I suppose, the original self-awareness and empowerment groups for women. Even before Elizabeth Cady Stanton and the others called the first Women's Rights Convention, Margaret was convening Boston women to challenge them to exercise their own thoughts and feelings and not just depend on the opinions of their husbands. Elizabeth Cady Stanton participated in one of Margaret's groups several years before the Seneca Falls convention. For the next half-century there were Fuller Clubs dedicated to this search for identity and freedom all over America and Europe. And it all began in my bookstore.

It was during some of these discussions that I first became acquainted with the ideas of the German educator Friedrich Froebel who had organized what he called Kindergartens in his native country.

In 1860 I took the best of his ideas, added some of my own, and organized the first Kindergarten in America. The rest of my life was spent expanding and extending the Kindergarten concept, based on the controlling idea of my life: The possibility of the nurture and full development of a child's – or any individual's – inherent capacity for good. What my dear friend and mentor Ellery Channing called "a likeness to God."

Good morning. I am
John Greenleaf Whittier

Most likely you think of me as a poet. While indeed I was, in my own eyes I was a crusader against slavery, a pacifist protester against war, and behind-the-scenes manipulator of politics and politicians.

I set a higher value on having my name appended to my 1833 anti-slavery manifesto, *Justice and Expediency*, than any verse I ever wrote or the title page of any book.

I was born in 1807 on a farm near Haverhill, Massachusetts to devout Quaker parents. I know it is said that I became a Unitarian, and I am not dismayed by that, but it was never so. Since, however, your Credos are open to both members and friends of your sect, I surely qualify as a friend.

I am a Quaker because my families before me – those whom I loved – were Quakers. I have held to Quaker customs and manners of speech throughout my life because these were my heritage.

I always found the Hicksite Quakers – that is, those of Unitarian-like beliefs as to the nature of God – more in keeping with my own thoughts. But in other ways I was most orthodox. I wished no music in our Meeting. I did not even want much speaking. All I wanted was to get into the silence.

If you have read the prefatory remarks to my poetic tribute to your William Ellery Channing, you will recall I separated myself from his "peculiar religious opinions." I agreed with the Unitarian anti-Calvinist stance against those who defamed them as heretics, but that was all.

William Lloyd Garrison published my first poetry in his Abolitionist Journal the *Free Press*. I later edited other anti-slavery papers, including the *National Era* in Washington when "Uncle Tom's Cabin" was first serialized.

I served for a period of time on the Massachusetts Legislature even though I never had any illusions about politics or politicians. But I did try to believe in them as long as possible and use them for causes I believed in after that.

In my early years I was affiliated with no political party. Most of the time my allegiance was to minority factions. But after the Civil War I remained true to the party of Lincoln for the rest of my life. Actually I voted for Lincoln four times. Twice at the polls and twice in the Electoral College.

Now you asked about my religious beliefs: I object to all creeds. Some of the worst forms of blasphemy are embodied in creeds, which good men try to persuade themselves that they believe.

As for the Bible, I wrote in "The Pennsylvania Pilgrim:"
Within himself he found the law of right
He walked by the faith and not by the letter's light
And read the Bible by the Inward Light.

Death? As I grew older a future life seemed to me more certain though I thought less and less of definite details. I could not conceive of an end to myself. I expected to live on, but how? I just knew that I had a constitutional dread of change or newness.

Spiritualism was much in vogue in my day. I had a number of friends who were very interested in it. Mrs. Child, Mrs. Stowe, Mrs. Thaxter, William Lloyd Garrison. I did, in fact, participate in séances with them. I had as good a chance to see a ghost as anyone else, but not the slightest sign ever came to me. Mrs. Child reported seeing one. I do not doubt what others tell me, but somehow wonder over my own incapacity. I would have liked for some dear ghost to have walked in and spoken with me.

One time the English Abolitionist George Thompson and I were set upon by an angry mob when we were conducting an anti-slavery rally in Concord, New Hampshire. They were determined to tar and feather us. Fortunately we were able to get to our carriage and escape.

Later I wrote a woman friend about the incident. "I was a hero. I was John Knox before the Catholic Queen – Martin Luther before the Pope's Council – I was George Fox before the mob of Castle Bosworth – William Penn before the bench of judges. Yea, verily of a Truth, I maintained the testimony and resisted not."

The truth is, of course, that I ran for my life. And, of course, she knew it.

The Civil War tested to the limit my commitment to pacifism. The Mexican War presented no such trial. It was wrong, and I never hesitated to declare it so. But this was a war to abolish slavery and had to be won by the Union. I therefore supported the North in every possible way other than taking arms, and encouraged all Quakers to do likewise.

It is ironic that I may be best remembered in your generation for my poetry, which has been set to the music of hymns. Remember me telling thee that I did not wish to have music at our times of sacred worship.

I note as well that thee has adapted, and improved on, the words I wrote in an earlier, quite different, century. Right here on page 274 of your songbook. Whereas I wrote "Dear Lord and Father of Mankind," you now sing, "Dear Mother-Father of us all."

That is a significant improvement, and I am pleased you have kept me current with evolving insights and enlightenment.

Good morning. I am
Charles Darwin

I have been asked to present my Credo; that is, speak about my religious beliefs.

Charles Darwin's religion? To many that probably sounds to be an oxymoron. Or, perhaps, they would expect seven minutes of Quaker-like silence.

But, in reality, after knowing what so many others have said about me, it is a pleasure to have the opportunity to speak for myself.

I spring from a background of British Unitarianism. My grandfather, the poet and philosopher Erasmus Darwin, said that "Unitarianism is a featherbed to catch a falling Christian." I suspect many of you can relate to that.

While on board the Beagle in my research voyages I remember being heartily laughed at by several officers and crewmen for quoting the Bible as an unanswerable authority on some point of morality. Not on science mind you, but on ethics.

Yet I had come, by this time, to see that the Old Testament with its manifestly false history of the world, the Tower of Babel, the rainbow as a sign, etc., etc., and its attributing to God the feelings of a revengeful tyrant, was no more to be trusted than the sacred books of the Hindoos or Muslims, or the beliefs of any barbarism.

Likewise I came to disbelieve in Christianity as a divine revelation. Beautiful as is the morality of the New Testament, it can hardly be denied that its perfection depends on the interpretation, which we now put on metaphors and allegories.

But I was never willing, or able, to give up my belief entirely. It is fair to say that I remained a Theist. I did not think much about a personal God. When reflecting I felt compelled to look to a First Cause having an intelligent mind in some degree analogous to that of man.

This conclusion was strong in my mind at the time I wrote, *Origin of Species*. I have never denied the possibility of a Creation, a First Cause. But I simply cannot pretend to throw light on such an abstruse problem. The mystery of the beginnings of all things is insoluble by us; and I, for one must be content to remain agnostic – not one who disbelieves, but one who does not know.

A person who has no assured and ever present belief in the existence of a personal God or of a future existence with retribution and reward, can have for his or her rule of life, as far as I can see, only to follow those impulses and instincts which are the strongest or which seem to him to be the best ones. A dog acts in this manner, but he does so blindly, so far as we can now ascertain. A person, on the other hand, looks forward and backward, compares various feelings, desires and recollections. He or she then finds, in accordance with the verdict of all the wisest of our human species, that the highest satisfaction is derived from following certain impulses, namely the social instincts.

By degrees it will become intolerable to obey sensuous passions rather than higher impulses, which, when rendered habitual, may be practically called instincts.

Reason may occasionally tell one to act in opposition to the opinions of others. Approbation will then be withheld. But that person will still have the satisfaction of having followed one's innermost guide or conscience.

As for myself, I believe I have acted rightly in steadily following and devoting my life to scientific research.

I cannot find remorse, as I do not believe I have committed great sin, but I have often regretted not having done more good for my fellow creatures.

What others may say about me or about the body of knowledge I have developed from my observations of the natural world is beyond my control and thus not worthy of my time or concern.

Nonetheless, I was amused by those little fish with the name DARWIN I saw on so many of your cars in the parking lot this morning.

Good morning. I am
Margaret Fuller

I was a member of that group of Boston intellectuals called Transcendentalists, the editor of their journal *The Dial*, the first woman editor of a major newspaper, and credited by many for having laid the groundwork for the feminist revolution in America. Born in Cambridgeport, Massachusetts in 1810, taught from the day of my birth by my father, Timothy Fuller, a lawyer and politician, and a member of the state Senate. He worked during the first half of the day and devoted the remaining hours to my education. By the time I was six I was reading Virgil, Horace and Ovid in the original Latin and was expected to translate into English without hesitation. That was just the beginning.

I was also born into a society, which did not readily accept deviation from the norm. It is hardly surprising, then, that I was resented for being more intelligent than most adults and certainly better educated than most boys. I am also sure that it did not help that false modesty was not one of my weaknesses. Waldo Emerson, with whom I had a remarkably positive working relationship for many years, once wrote that I was possessed of a "mountainous me."

In my early twenties I joined Amos Bronson Alcott as a teacher at his experimental school in Boston. It was called "Temple School" because it was located above the Masonic Temple. It was then that I became acquainted with Emerson, with Horace Mann, with Henry Thoreau and with Channing and all of the others who were in the Transcendental Club. I was one of the few women accepted into this group, but I was never their handmaiden. Because I was better versed in literary criticism than any of the others, I was chosen to edit *The Dial*.

After only two years of operation the Temple School was forced to close. It was simply too progressive to be accepted by the public. Elizabeth Peabody, who had also taught at the school, opened the West Street Bookshop in Boston, and opened to me the opportunity to pursue a major passion in my life.

At Temple School we had taught through the conversational method. We did not cram facts into the heads of the children, but, rather, involved them in creative conversation, which allowed them to grow from within.

I established Conversation Groups for women at Elizabeth's bookstore. There were thirteen weekly sessions permitting women to explore their own inner lives, to be free in expressing their own thoughts and feelings, and to enjoy the intellectual stimulation of other women.

In 1839, a decade before Elizabeth Cady Stanton and others convened the first Women's Rights Convention in Seneca Falls, I convened a group of twenty-five distinguished New England women.

That was the first of thousands of similar Fuller Clubs that met across America and in Europe. Mrs. Stanton, by the way, was one of the early participants.

In addition to the Conversations, I published in *The Dial* "The Great Lawsuit: Man Versus Woman, Woman Versus Man." It was a true trailblazer in the cause of women's rights. I maintained that a woman must fulfill herself as an individual apart from any relationship with a man. Not to do so is to remain an "overgrown child." What a woman needs is not to rule; but as a nature to grow, as an intellect to discern, as a soul to live freely; and, unimpeded, to unfold such powers as were given her when we left our common home.

The article created a sensation. For the first time an issue of the magazine sold out. Horace Greeley, editor of the New York Tribune, the nation's most progressive newspaper, read the article.

His wife had earlier attended one of my Conversations. Together they agreed that I should have a wider readership and, to attract more women subscribers, the *Tribune*, should be the paper. I was offered the position as Assistant Editor, which I accepted without hesitation. Horace Greeley, by the way, was a Unitarian, as were almost all of my Boston friends and colleagues.

"Man Versus Woman" was reprinted as a book by the *Tribune* under the title *Woman in the Nineteenth Century*. It quickly became one of the most talked about books of the day and a virtual Bible for the emerging feminist movement.

Since you asked me to talk about my person religious beliefs, I had best give some attention to that. I was a Unitarian, but was never satisfied. If all had been like my friend and mentor William Ellery Channing, it would have been different, but he was an exception. One summer I took an extended trip into Northern Michigan and the Wisconsin Territory. In the journal I kept of that trip I noted: If Boston's Unitarian ministers offend me by their dull and literal-minded sermons, how much more offensive to me is the hypocrisy of the missionaries who are robbing the Indians of their culture and religion and offering them in return nothing but subservience and degradation of spirit.

My Credo can be found somewhere in that observation.

Good morning, I am
Theodore Parker

In 1838, when I was twenty-nine years old, and two years into my Unitarian ministry, I heard Ralph Waldo Emerson deliver his famous Divinity School Address at Harvard. I was so overwhelmed by the beauty, truth and courage of his words that I determined it was time for me to begin to speak more openly and honestly in my pulpit about my most cherished beliefs.

Shortly thereafter, in an ordination sermon for a fellow clergyman in South Boston, I preached on "The Transient and the Permanent in Christianity." Miracles, revelations, creeds and doctrines are transient. The only permanence is the moral sense discovered intuitively by people of goodwill. Jesus was a moral guide, but not a god.

That may not sound very radical or revolutionary to you, but most of my Unitarian brethren were stunned and outraged. A delegation from the Boston Unitarian Ministers Association visited me to request that I resign.

At that moment I envisioned how, as a lad of fourteen my father had stood near the village green in 1775 and heard my grandfather, Captain John Parker, say to his Lexington Minute Men: "If they mean to have a war, let is start here."

I refused to resign. I told them they would have to formally expel me, if that was their desire; but I would never voluntarily accept restrictions on my right to speak the truth as I perceived it. They never pursued the matter further.

I grew up on a farm, which had been in our family for over one hundred years. All of my remembrances are of a very happy childhood. I am told that my blessed mother, Hannah, indulged me in ways so different from traditional Puritan parenthood that the neighbors were scandalized.

I am sure it was her loving influence which prompted me to emphasize the feminine and nurturing side of God's nature in my earliest preaching. I preached and prayed both the Fatherhood and Motherhood of God more than a century and a half ago. Many of my ministerial brethren thought this further proof of a hopeless heresy.

The Unitarians of my day, you see, had followed Channing out of the Congregational Church twenty years earlier on the basis of their opposition to Trinitarianism and the Calvinist concept of a God of vengeance and retribution. But they had not been willing to go one step beyond that. Their cry was "Duty! Duty! Work! Work!" But they could not bring themselves to shout, "Joy! Joy! Joy!" They had ceased to fear, but could not yet truly love. The kindly Dr. Channing, of course, was an exception.

A few years later I settled with the Twenty-eighth Society and preached weekly in a large Boston ballroom, The Melodeon. We regularly saw seven thousand in attendance. The largest congregation in New England, I was told.

The congregation had an unusual number of working class persons and recent immigrants. They did not always conduct themselves with the decorum upper class Unitarians could approve. Dr. Samuel Howe was one of my closest friends and though we worked together on a number of important humanitarian causes, he would not permit his wife or children to attend my services. His wife, Julia Ward Howe, did frequently attend evening services alone, however.

Opposition to slavery was the other passion of my life. It was for me a religious imperative. To hold another in bondage was to deny the God in whose image each slave had been created. Early I joined William Lloyd Garrison, even though he was held in contempt by most of the clergy. He was too direct, too rough, too zealous to suit their more genteel tastes.

I castigated Boston's idol, Daniel Webster, for his support of the Fugitive Slave Act, which he thought was a way to appease the South. I actively participated in the Underground Railroad. When the Fugitive Slave Law passed, I assumed leadership of the Committee of Vigilance, which was organized to keep runaway slaves from being caught and returned to the South.

On one occasion, two paid agents appeared in Boston to capture William and Ellen Craft, two fugitive slaves who were my parishioners. I took a delegation to the hotel where the bounty hunters were staying, told them of the great danger they were in because of public outrage at their actions, and offered to escort them to the train station so they could make a safe getaway. They refused my offer, but two hours later they left – never to return.

I raised funds for John Brown in response to his request for help with a secret mission, which turned out to be his raid on the armory at Harper's Ferry. For that I was summoned to Washington by a Senate investigating committee.

I suppose the essence of my Credo is in the appeal I always made to young people to take possession of the churches, to make them instruments of practical religion for the common people. A church of old men goes to its grave, a church of young men goes to its work!

Good morning. I am
Henry David Thoreau

Let's clarify one thing right at the beginning. I was asked to share with you today my personal credo – a statement of my religious or spiritual beliefs. I will attempt to do that. But you need to understand that I was never a Unitarian.

Oh yes, all of my closest friends were Unitarians, and I certainly share those beliefs which separate the Unitarians from the Calvinists, but I was never a church-going man. I understand that the Unitarians, for some reason I will never comprehend, have tried to claim me. But, I couldn't have been a member even if I wanted to. On principle I always refused to pay the required Church Tax, and that eliminated me automatically. Now, is that matter cleared?

I was born in Concord, Massachusetts in 1817 to a family with French and Scottish bloodlines and Quaker and Puritan religious heritage. My father was a pencil maker, and I worked periodically in this enterprise.

I attended Harvard University and graduated in the class of 1837. I did little to distinguish myself as a scholar and seldom participated in campus activities. I did present a paper at Commencement in which I questioned God's judgment in decreeing that man should labor for six days and rest on the seventh. I thought it better if man could work to earn his bread on one day and experience the Sabbath on the other six.

The primary value of my years at Harvard was the fact that I studied under the rhetorician E.T. Channing, fell under the spell of Emerson, and became friends with Bronson Alcott, Nathaniel

Hawthorne, and Margaret Fuller. I was accepted as the youngest member of the Transcendantalist Club.

After graduation I accepted a teaching position. After only two weeks, however, I was reprimanded by the School Board for not having caned any students. Corporal punishment, they said, was a necessary part of a teacher's responsibilities. I resigned, and that was the end of my teaching.

I worked at odd jobs rather than getting tied down to any full time responsibility. Particularly appealing was surveying, at which I was quite adept, and which permitted me to be out-of-doors and in touch with the real world.

On July 4, 1845 I borrowed an axe from my neighbor Bronson Alcott, and walked two miles outside of Concord to the banks of Walden Pond. On land owned by Waldo Emerson I built a small cabin at the total cost of $26.12. For the next two years I lived there in splendid isolation; fishing, trapping, gathering berries for my food. I had a small garden plot. My needs were so few that my weekly expenditure amounted to twenty-six cents.

I lost myself in the observation of nature. Every plant, every animal, every change of the wind or formation of cloud in the sky became my laboratory. I faithfully recorded every seasonal change, every change in the water in the pond, and noted its effect on every form of wildlife.

It was here, also, I wrote my first book, a travel narrative of a float trip down the Concord and Merrimack Rivers which I had taken with my brother the summer before.

My two years experience in isolation at Walden Pond led, of course, to my best-known book *Walden: Or Life in the Woods*.

Let's see, what can I tell you about myself? I was a surveyor. That was my only wage earning endeavor. But I was also an ecologist, a hydrographer, an ichthyologist, a botanist, and a taxonomist by personal preference.

I never really felt at home with people, preferring solitude, and distrusting intimacy. Emerson was my friend and mentor. He provided me lodging in his home, and twice I resided with his family while he was away on extended journeys. If there was any person with whom I felt comfortable it was Emerson. Yet he once said of me, "As for taking his arm, I should as soon think of taking the arm of an elm tree."

When Congress passed the Missouri Compromise I refused to pay my taxes because I believed the government was furthering the expansion of slavery. I was arrested and jailed. This led to the publication of my treatise on "Civil Disobedience" in which I argued that the person of conscience had a duty to refuse to obey unjust laws.

Now, you wanted to know what I believe. Here is a bit of it.

"Beware of all enterprises that require new clothes."

"Do not think that you can kill time without injuring eternity."

"Rather than love, or money, or fame, give me truth."

"Every man is tasked to make his life, even in its details, worthy of the contemplation of his most elevated and critical hour."

"Never be afraid to march to the beat of your own drummer."

Finally, and most important:

"Simply, Simply! Simplify!"

Good morning, I am
Julia Ward Howe

I am probably best known to you as having written the words for the "Battle Hymn of the Republic." I assure you, songwriting was incidental to a very interesting and productive life.

That life was shared, molded, frustrated and enhanced by two strong and influential men. My father, Samuel Ward, was the banker of great fortune and business acumen who was credited with saving the city of New York from bankruptcy in the Panic of 1837 during my 17th year. He was also a strict Calvinist who put stern restrictions on the activities of his family. I loved him dearly and resented him deeply for his interference with my social aspirations.

The other man was my husband, Samuel Gridley Howe. Nearly twenty years my senior, Sam was a physician of international renown, the leading pioneer in treatment of the blind here and in Europe and an ardent abolitionist, a philanthropist and supporter of almost every liberal cause of the 19th century. Though a great advocate of women's rights in general, he balked at supporting those tenets in his own wife. He tried to prohibit publication of an early volume of my poetry and discouraged my involvement in social causes. Even after I had challenged his authority and achieved considerable recognition as a lecturer and leader of liberal causes, he was never reconciled to my involvement.

I both admired and adored the man. We were husband and wife for 35 years, until his death. Yet, sometime in the middle years of our union, I wrote in my journal: "Marriage, like death, is a debt a woman owes to nature."

Another man who had great influence on me, though in quite a different vein than father or husband, was Theodore Parker, the most radical of the Unitarian preachers of Boston. My husband was a friend of Parker through the network of the Transcendentalists – Emerson, Alcott, the Longfellow brothers and the others.

Yet, despite this friendship he strongly disapproved of my regular attendance at Parker's church. Unlike other elitist Unitarians, Parker had a congregation of the working class and immigrants and he was fearless in preaching against the rich. Sam thought my attendance reflected poorly on himself. My compromise was to take the children to a fashionable church on Sunday mornings, then go to hear Parker preach on Sunday evenings.

Though I did not officially join the Unitarian Church until several years later, it was what I heard from Parker together with my readings of Spinoza, Hegel and Schelling, that helped me develop a creed which I could rightly call my own. My mind was freed from the strictures of my Calvinistic upbringing. I came to understand that the spirit of the liberal church lies not so much in what we believe as in the manner in which we believe it. Thus, I came to understand that Christianity was not an exclusive avenue to God, but only one of God's many plans for bringing humanity to a state of ultimate perfection.

You may have difficulty in reconciling my concept of an all-loving Deity with the words I wrote for the "Battle Hymn." I confess that, in retrospect, I do as well.

> *"He is trampling out the vintage where the grapes of wrath are stored;*
> *He has loosed the fateful lightening of His terrible swift sword*
> *His truth is marching on!"*

All I can say is that, during the war, when I was so totally immersed in the cause of saving the Union and freeing the slaves, I, at least emotionally, reverted to the vengeful and judgmental God of my childhood. It seemed so appropriate at the time.

When the war was over I threw myself into other causes. I

had long avoided involvement with the Women's Rights Movement, foolishly thinking it too strident and not feminine. But, I was won over by Lucy Stone whom I found I had badly misjudged. I became president of the New England Suffrage Association and worked with Stone for two decades in the moderate wing of the Suffrage movement. Opposed, that is, to the radical wing headed by Susan B. Anthony and Elizabeth Cady Stanton.

The Franco-Prussian War of 1870 resurrected awful memories of our own Civil War. I was determined then that, just as my Battle Hymn had roused the fighting spirit of the North, I would find a new instrument to arouse a spirit of peace throughout the world.

To that end I founded the Women's International Peace Association. A special Sunday was set aside for the mothers of the world to mobilize for peace. This was the beginning of the annual observance of Mother's Day. But its original purpose was something quite other than greeting cards, flowers and candy.

As I dedicated the rest of my life to the quest for world peace, it seemed to me, all avenues of my lifelong search for a meaningful liberal religion had come together.

In my final year my daughter asked me the purpose of life. I told her, as I tell you now:

"To Learn. To Teach. To Serve. And to Enjoy!"

Good morning. I am
Susan B. Anthony

My assignment this morning, as I understand it, it to share with you something of my personal belief and religious journey.

That is not an easy task because I don't know what religion is. I only know what work is, and that is all I can speak on, this side of Jordan. Work is my gospel. It is what I believe in.

When I heard you recite together your Aspiration, and say "Service is our prayer", I knew I was among kindred spirits. I said essentially the same thing in 1896 when a reporter asked if I ever prayed. I told him: "I pray every second of my life; not on my knees, but with my work. My prayer is to lift women to equality with men. Work and worship are one with me. I know there is no God of the universe made happy by me getting down on my knees and telling him how great he is."

I was born and raised a Quaker, a member of the Society of Friends. My father was an ardent Abolitionist and our home in Rochester, New York was the central meeting place for those involved in the anti-slavery crusade. Not just local people, but also famous leaders of the movement when they were in the Rochester area.

As the nation reached the mid-point of the century it seemed inevitable that slavery could only be abolished through a Civil War. This forced the Quakers into a painful dilemma. The Friends were pacifists, opposed to all violence and war. They were opposed to slavery, which, it seemed, could only be abolished through violence. Most resolved this dilemma by giving primary attention to keeping slavery from expanding to the new states in the West. They believed that if oppression could be contained it might eventually wither and die by itself.

My father and I took a more radical position, believing that slavery must be abolished and by whatever means necessary. We then joined the Unitarian Society in Rochester where Frederick Douglass worshipped and where the minister was Samuel May, the most outspoken Abolitionist among the Unitarian clergy.

I remained Unitarian for the rest of my life, but never ceased considering myself a Quaker. There was simply too much of me in each of these movements to deny the reality of either.

While I was on the road campaigning for Women's Rights, which was most of the time, I seldom attended religious services. As I said, work and worship were the same to me. But whenever I was back home in Rochester, I seldom missed a service. I looked forward to my Sunday Uplift.

Many of my good friends, supporters and co-workers, were members of the clergy, but my relationship with organized religion as a whole was somewhat less than friendly. They did not hesitate to brand me as a dangerous infidel, and I had little hesitancy in expressing my intolerance for the hypocrisy of most of the organized sects.

One of the things that upset many people, including some of my closest friends, was the fact that I was adamant that we always had to find room for everyone under the suffragist tent. As long as a person agreed on the vote, the holy of holies, I didn't worry about anything else.

In the early years of our struggle I fought to make sure that the very religious did not exclude those they considered irreligious.

Later on the challenge was to keep was to keep the irreligious from excluding the religionists. I told our convention in 1890 that I was ready to fight for another forty years "to make our platform free for the Christian to stand on, whether she be a Catholic who counts her beads, or a Protestant of the most orthodox sect; just as I have fought for the rights of the infidels the last forty years. These are the principals I want to maintain – that our platform be kept as broad as the universe, that upon it may stand those of all creeds, and no creeds – Jew and Christian, Protestant and Catholic, Mormon, Gentile, believer, atheist."

In 1892, at the Columbian Exposition in Chicago, I was invited to address the Religious Press Convention. What a rich irony! They assigned me the topic, "The Moral Leadership of the Religious Press." In brief, here is what I told them:

For one who for fifty years has been ridiculed by both press and pulpit, denounced as infidel by both, to be invited to speak here is, to say the least, very funny. Nevertheless I am happy to stand here as an object lesson on the survival of the fittest, from ridicule and contempt.

I was born into this earth in the midst of division of the Society of Friends on the great question which has divided all the religious people of Christendom. I took the radical side, the Unitarian, which you in the press denounced as infidel.

I passed through the experience of three great reforms – temperance, the anti-slavery movement and the woman question. The religious press, instead of being a leader in any of these great moral reforms, has usually lagged behind. Many of you have taken great pride in scarifying Miss Anthony. Now that I am seventy-three years old, you are all rushing to praise me.

After that, they gave me a great ovation. To use a very contemporary phrase, Go figure!

Good morning. I am
Mary Rice Livermore

I was born in north Boston in the year 1820, fourth of the six children of Timothy and Zebia Rice. My father was an old-fashioned Calvinist Baptist. Mother was of the same faith, but was less rigid in her adherence to its tenets.

In our household there was Bible reading and prayer at every meal. Each night, before bedtime prayers, each of us was expected to give father an account of our use of every hour of the the day.

From the age of six, each of us was required to read the entire Bible every year.

In many ways father was a good-hearted and caring man, but he was so weighted down by his Calvinistic beliefs that any light-heartedness or joy was short-lived. His constant prayer was that his children would escape the endless punishment he believed would be the fate of most of the human race.

All of this was most disturbing to me. I was convinced from the beginning that I would be among the damned. My only image of God was as a stern and uncaring judge, who put people on trial, condemned or acquitted them, and sent them to heaven or, more likely, to hell. I wanted to reject all of this, but could not do so. My girlhood compromise was to continue my prayers, but to address them to "Our Jesus, who art in heaven" – a less frightening figure.

At the age of sixteen, after graduating from Charlestown Female Academy, I was offered a position as tutor to the children of a wealthy plantation family in Virginia. Father was opposed to my leaving home, believing that a woman should remain under her father's roof until she was given in marriage to another man. For the first time in my life I defied him and accepted the position in the South. While I enjoyed the children and teaching them, I was horrified by what I saw of human slavery. Up to this time I had no strong feelings on the subject, one way or the other. But after seeing it with my own eyes, I became a dedicated abolitionist.

After fulfilling my three-year contract, I returned to Massachusetts and found a teaching position in Duxbury.

On a Christmas Eve walk I passed by a Universalist Church. I heard carols being sung which sounded so much more joyous than I had ever heard in church. Our church in Boston did not permit any celebration of Christmas, believing it to be a Catholic (therefore, pagan) holiday.

I don't know what drew me in. I certainly had no such intention when I began my walk. But I found myself inside, listening to a sermon by a young minister such as I had never heard before. It was a message about the love of God, about the Good Shepard who never rests until every lost sheep is safely in the fold. For the first time in my life I was comforted rather than frightened by a church service. I'll quickly skip the immediate follow-up to tell you that one year later this village schoolteacher married that young Universalist minister and became Mrs. Daniel Livermore.

During the next decade we moved often. Daniel and I both were outspoken advocates of the abolition of slavery, and in every parish there were those who wished to forbid their minister to speak on that subject.

In 1858 we moved to Chicago where Daniel became the editor of a Universalist magazine.

I threw myself into both church and community work, helping to found the Chicago Home for Aged Women, and the Hospital for Women and Children. I did some work as a reporter and was the only woman with press credentials at the convention which nominated Abraham Lincoln for the presidency.

During the Civil War I was appointed to the United States Sanitary Commission, a body responsible for the welfare and relief of soldiers. I raised money. I arranged for supplies to be sent to the front. I visited military camps to supervise the distribution of clothing and medical supplies and brought the sick and wounded back to northern hospitals.

Service on that wartime Commission convinced me, based on my personal observations, that a large portion of this nation's work was badly done, or not done at all; and that a major reason for that was the fact that women were excluded from the public arena. This awakened in me a new political consciousness, and led me to become much more actively involved in the Woman Suffrage movement.

I established and edited *The Agitiator* in Chicago, which later merged with *The Woman's Journal,* a weekly published in Boston. I became editor-in-chief and Daniel and I moved back to Massachusetts where we resided for the rest of our lives.

I had a long and fulfilling life. Early misconceptions darkened my childhood and youth, but the discovery of Universalism made all the difference. It is the central thing in my being. So, this is my Credo: I believe in a loving God, and have an abiding faith in human destiny.

Good morning. I am
Clara Barton

I am going to assume that you are familiar with my works as a battlefield nurse during the Civil War and my subsequent founding of the American Red Cross. I see no reason to retrace that territory here today.

You have invited me to speak about my religious beliefs. Once before I was asked by a newspaper reporter to do that, and I refused. It was simply not possible for me to speak off the cuff on such a complicated and profound subject. But since you have given me a little time to prepare, I will do my best to comply with your request.

I grew up in the Universalist Church in Oxford, Massachusetts. My parents were founding members of the congregation, and we never missed a service.

After leaving home I attended a variety of denominations, principally Universalist, Congregational and Unitarian. They all had so much in common that I thought it a shame they did not unite as one.

As a Universalist I believed in the goodness and loving-kindness of God. I was not really a Unitarian because I believed in the divinity of Jesus; but it was a divinity of preeminence and not of exclusion. That is, it seemed to me that Jesus became the Son of God by moral processes, which are essentially within the reach of all people. We are all created in the image of God, and each of us has the same potential to become a divine Beloved Son or Daughter.

But such theological distinctions seemed rather insignificant to me. I know that when I cradled a wounded soldier in my arms, prayed with him and shared with him my faith in God's love and universal immortality, all those other matters were of little consequence whatsoever.

It was widely rumored, when I was in my later years, that I had gone over to Christian Science. This was not so. I did study the work of Mary Baker Eddy and had great respect for her. I thought it a quite remarkable thing that she had been able to accomplish so much – a woman alone against such great opposition.

I was further interested in her teaching about the relationship between faith and health. I had certainly seen too much reckless use of medicine and needless surgery. Both in war and in peace I saw much use of the surgeon's scalpel that seemed to me to be both bloody and cruel. I was long aware that people who take medicine usually take too much. That a cheerful and wholesome attitude toward life is usually better than medicine.

But having said this, let me assure you I never refused medical attention for my own needs, I employed physicians to the end of my days. But all the while I also knew that spiritual things are real and that a person is more than a body.

My efforts to find that which was good in Christian Science were sincere; but those experiments did not make me a Christian Scientist.

At the core of my system of belief was a faith in immortality. That faith was so strong that some thought I was a Spiritualist. I don't believe that was ever so. But I did believe that those whom I had loved and lost were still very near to me. I felt they exerted an influence over me. Particularly my brother, Stephen, who died in the Civil War – and my mother, who was always with me. If that makes me a Spiritualist, so be it. I just never thought myself to be one.

While preparing for this assignment I came upon two letters, which may help you understand my religious beliefs a little better. Let me read you an excerpt from each of them.

The first is to a niece of mine who was being assaulted by the religious revivalists and didn't quite know how to handle them. I sent her a copy of a fine sermon by a sound Unitarian clergyman who does not believe in special revivals of religion, as gotten up for the occasions and to fill churches, but thinks religion, as being the best part of man's nature, will revive itself like all else in nature, and feels that God does not need to be implored to save from endless pain and loss the poor creatures He has made, but believes that if we do our best to enlighten and elevate those around us we do all we are called upon to do in the way of their salvation. "Take your time, my dear. Read and consider, and don't either fall into a trap or be driven into one. Selah!"

Then in my 90th year, I wrote the following to Judge A.W. Terrell in Austin, Texas:

"I suppose I am not what the world denominates a church woman. I lay no claim to it. I was born to liberal views, and have lived a liberal creed. I firmly believe in the divinity of Jesus of Nazareth – but it would be difficult for me to stop there and believe that this spark of divinity was accorded to none other of God's creation, who like the Master, took on the living form, and, like him, lived the human life."

Good morning. I am
Edward Everett Hale

You may recognize me as the author of *The Man Without A Country* but you might be surprised to learn that I was a Unitarian minister for more than six decades. From 1841 to 1903, to be precise. Most of those years were spent at South Church in Boston.

I take pride in having been one of the leaders of the so-called "Broad Church" group, which put the Unitarian denomination on a more solid organizational footing with the establishment of the National Conference of Unitarian Churches in 1865.

The Unitarians, you see, who had become a denomination in 1825 with the creation of the American Unitarian Association were in danger of splitting apart. The "right wing" held fast to traditional Christian beliefs while the "left wing" wanted to break free from its Christian roots entirely. Others of us, particularly Henry Bellows and I, believed that rather than being a nighthawk with two huge wings, we were really more like an ostrich with a broad body and two small wings. Hence the "Broad Church" designation.

My roots in New England ran deep. I was directly related to the American patriot Nathan Hale, and to the Boston political leader Edward Everett. From these two, of course, came my name. I received my education at Harvard College, and then taught for three years at the Boston Latin School. During this period I also prepared myself for the ministry through supervised private study, which I always thought was superior to any formal Divinity training I could possibly have received.

The Divinity School at Harvard was undergoing some very

harsh critical review at the time. Theodore Parker, one of the most influential voices in the growth of liberal religious thought in our history, compared the Divinity School faculty to morticians.

"Egyptian embalmers," he said, "took only seventy days to make a mummy out of a dead man, whereas Unitarian embalmers at Harvard use three years in making mummies out of men." Yes, my choice of "reading divinity" with a season clergyman rather than attending seminary was a wise one.

The early years of my ministry were predictably ordinary. I was an energetic minister in an active church, but my influence did not reach beyond that local congregation.

Then two things happened, almost simultaneously, and thrust me into the public arena. I was never to return to the simple parish life again. One was my leadership in organizing the National Conference, which necessitated considerable travel and lecturing. The second was the publication of the story I mentioned earlier.

I always did my best preaching by telling stories, and the publication of many of those tales certainly extended the influence of my pulpit. Even better known than *The Man Without A Country* was a story named *Ten Times One is Ten*, which was published in 1870. Its optimistic message was "Look up and not down! Look out and not in! Look forward and not back! And, lend a hand!"

Lend-A-Hand Clubs were formed all over the country as people grasped onto this popular message of forward looking and progressive liberalism.

When I retired at the age of eighty-one, I was appointed Chaplain to the United States Senate. When they asked me to accept that assignment I was told that my job was to pray for the Senators at the opening of each session. What I really did was look over that chamber full of Senators and pray for my country.

My credo? It can all be found in that story *Ten Times One is Ten*. I believed it then and I have never faltered in that belief. Always look up and not down! Look out and not in! Look forward and not back! And always, always, always, lend a hand!

Good Morning, I am
Thomas Starr King

I have never been called by my first name and have always been known as Starr. I was born in 1824 in New York City, the child of a popular and prominent Universalist minister.

There seems to have never been any question that I would follow in his vocational footsteps and my first sermon was published when I was only thirteen years of age.

There was only one thing to temper my parent's joy and pride at my precociousness – and that was an impish sense of humor. How could a congregation respect a minister who saw the ludicrousness in almost every situation, and enjoyed it thoroughly? I'll admit that, at times, I wondered the same.

My father died when I was fifteen and financial responsibility for my family was suddenly thrust upon me. All thoughts of college education and seminary training were forced aside. As you can see, I was small in stature, hardly more than five feet tall. Thus, many forms of manual labor were simply beyond my physical abilities. But I did find work as a bookkeeper at the Navy Yard in Charlestown, Massachusetts, where the family had moved several years earlier.

The proximity to Harvard frequently gave me the opportunity to attend lectures at that great university, though I never officially enrolled. When I was twenty-one a small Universalist church called this graduate of the Charlestown Navy Yard to be its minister. A couple of years later I was called to the Hollis Street Unitarian Society in Boston. In making this shift of denomination

I was not repudiating Universalism. To the contrary, it was simply an indication that my faith had grown to incorporate Unitarian beliefs as well. As I explained at the time, there seemed to me to be very little difference between the Universalists and the Unitarians. The Universalists believe that God is too good to damn anyone forever, and the Unitarians believe they are too good to be damned forever.

Now, do you understand why my parents worried that some might find me too flippant to be a successful clergyman?

Even though I had been ordained by the Universalists despite my limited formal education, the Unitarians took a chance. Two years later, satisfied with my performance, Harvard granted me an honorary degree of Master of Arts.

In 1860 I made the momentous decision to leave my beloved Boston for two years to minister to the newly formed Unitarian Society in San Francisco. That rowdy, rambunctious, tumultuous city by the Bay, which, in the twelve years since the discovery of gold in California, had become the foremost city on the Pacific coast.

The 1860 presidential election was tearing the new state of California asunder. There was a four way split. The Republican candidate was Abraham Lincoln. Northern Democrats supported Stephen Douglass, while the Southern wing of the party had nominated John Breckenridge of Kentucky. A sizable number of citizens wanted to wash their hands of it all and declare California an independent Pacific Republic.

Less than a month after I arrived in San Francisco I made a speech in which I declared myself foursquare behind the Union, the Republican Party and Abraham Lincoln. Suddenly I became the spiritual leader of those who sympathized with the North even though it seemed at that time that those who favored the expansion of slavery into California held the upper hand.

From that moment through the November election I traveled widely and campaigned ceaselessly for the cause of the Union. When the ballots were cast, Lincoln won California's four electoral votes. I was hailed, perhaps unduly, as the man who had saved

California for the Union. I was offered an opportunity to represent the state in the United States Senate, but refused. I was not a politician. I was a minister. My involvement in that campaign was motivated by the ethical requirements of my religious faith. My mission was to establish and further the cause of liberal religion on the Pacific Coast.

I had originally agreed to serve in San Francisco for a period of two years. My congregation in Boston had granted a leave-of-absence for that period. But there was too much to be done in California. A new building, seating 1500, to be built on Geary Street in San Francisco; the establishment of new congregations in Seattle, Portland, and several other California communities.

We purchased the organ for the new building through a series of lectures I presented dealing with prominent, living American poets. Bryant, Longfellow, Holmes, Whittier and Lowell – Unitarians every one – each wrote an original poem for the series. This represented a major step in my dream of transforming San Francisco from a frontier outpost to the Boston of the west.

By 1864 my health had broken. Diphtheria was followed by pneumonia, and I died when I was only thirty-nine. I've heard there is a statue of me in Golden Gate Park and a mountain named after me in the Sierras.

Good morning. I am
Antoinette Brown Blackwell.

Reverend Antoinette Brown Blackwell to be exact. My friends call me Nettie. I was born in Henrietta, New York in 1825.

Our family faithfully attended the Congregational Church in that village. I was only eight years old when a guest minister at our church pointed his finger at the crowd – I thought he was pointing directly at me – and asked "Have you decided how you will give your life to God? I want you to think deeply on this matter during the next week and be prepared to answer next Sunday."

I thought very much about it all week, and when our Sunday School teacher asked the following Sunday, I told her I wanted to be a minister.

"You can't do that, Nettie. Girls can't be ministers."

"But why?"

"There are no buts about it, Nettie. Girls just cannot be ministers."

When I told my mother about this, she gave me a big hug and told me that she had never heard of a girl becoming a minister, either, but that if that was my dream it might come true.

That night I decided I would need something with me at all times to remind me of that dream – something I could hold on to when others criticized or failed to understand. So I took a small piece of white ribbon and pinned it inside my collar.

It took seventeen years, but I was never a single day without that white ribbon. I completed my theological studies at Oberlin University in 1850, when I was twenty-five years of age. But the Congregational Church denied me a license because I was a woman. A year later they partially relented and permitted me to preach, but still withheld full ordination rites.

I became active in the Temperance Movement and in the struggle to free the slaves. I also had the opportunity to become closely acquainted with Elizabeth Cady Stanton, Susan B. Anthony, Lucretia Mott, Lucy Stone and others in the newborn movement for women's rights. In fact, I later became a sister-in-law of Lucy Stone. We both married into the Blackwell family. That was surely one of the most remarkable families in American history.

The two Blackwell brothers, Henry and Samuel, were leaders in the Abolitionist cause. Their sister, Elizabeth, was the first woman physician in America. Lucy Stone, who married Henry, was the first woman graduate of an American university and a co-convener of the first Woman's Rights Convention. I, who married Samuel, was the first woman minister.

Shortly after my marriage I wrote my friend Susan B. Anthony expressing the wish that there were a third Blackwell brother for her to marry. Susan was not at all pleased by my suggestion.

At the time of my marriage I joined my husband in the Unitarian Church. Again, I was denied full ordination, but was "recognized" as a Unitarian minister.

One of my major interests was the relation of theology to modern science. In 1875 I published *The Sexes Throughout Nature*, a feminist critique of the evolutionary theories of Darwin and Spencer. In that book I argued forcefully that nature indicated the equality of the sexes throughout the species.

I organized the Unitarian Church in Elizabeth, New Jersey and served there for many years.

I remained an ardent advocate for women's rights throughout my life. By living to be ninety-six, I was the only one of the early suffragists who was still around to cast a vote when women were finally permitted at the polls in 1920.

You asked me to share with you what I believe? I believe in dreaming your highest dream and staying with it until it all becomes true.

You see, I never took off that white ribbon. Here it is pinned beneath my collar. It is a great way to be reminded to keep your dreams alive. It not only worked for me, but others as well.

Olympia Brown, who was not related, though we shared the same last name, was ten years my junior. She dreamed of becoming a minister in the Universalist Church. As a student at Antioch College she arranged to have me preach at a Chapel service. She related to me her dreams and her frustrations, reciting all the obstacles, which were being placed in her path. I showed her my white ribbon and explained its significance to her. We found another piece of cloth and fashioned a ribbon for her. I pinned it on her dress. She was still wearing it when she was ordained in the Universalist Church, the first woman officially ordained by any religious body in America.

Good morning. I am
Louisa May Alcott

My guess is that every person here today is already familiar with my Credo. If you have read *Little Women*, as I suspect you have, you know my story. Meg was my older sister Anna. Beth was my younger sister Lizzie. Amy was the baby of the family, my little sister Abby May. And Jo? That was me! A writer is supposed to write about what she knows. And what I knew best was my family. Everything I believe and hold dear is embraced in the pages of that book.

I was born in Germantown, Pennsylvania in 1832. My father was the philosopher Amos Bronson Alcott. Along with Ralph Waldo Emerson and Henry David Thoreau, father was associated with a group of idealistic intellectuals called Transcendentalists.

Father organized a school in Boston based on very progressive principles of education. He believed that a child's "divine nature" could be "awakened" by dialogue between teacher and pupil. He taught in that wise way which develops what lies in a child's nature, much as a flower blooms, rather than stuffing the child with more than it could contain like a Strasburg goose. He believed that question and answer sessions could unfold truths and insights already within the child.

He also introduced sex education in his Temple School – and enrolled a black student – which was too much for Boston and angry parents shut the school down. So, we moved to Concord to start over again.

Father was a tender man. He was, of course, my model for Mr.

March. He loved to play with my sisters and me. Every night he told us stories. He encouraged us to make up stories of our own, and praised us highly when we did so. His early urging that I write poetry and plays and keep a daily journal surely had much to do with my later success as a writer.

Yet, my father was not a practical man in the marketplace. He dreamed great dreams, saw them fail one after another, but never stopped dreaming.

When I was ten years old father and another of his Unitarian friends, Charles Lane, organized an experimental farm community named Fruitland. They believed in the possibility of human perfectibility, and felt it could be achieved through self-discipline and self-sacrifice. Fruitland was to be the place where this belief about human potential could be realized. The farm would provide the communal environment where people could live and work together in harmony, peace and love.

We lived there with a number of families, and it offered many good experiences. But it was a difficult and spartan existence. We ate no meat, for the community believed it wrong to take the life of another creature. We wore only rough linen clothing because it would have been wrong to even take the woolen coat from a sheep, or cotton which was the product of the exploitation of slaves.

The Fruitland experiment failed after only three years, and the family moved back to a house in Concord given to us by Ralph Waldo Emerson. It was this experience that set my goal in life – to help my family from their life of poverty.

In the following years I taught school, worked as a domestic, and during the Civil War I served as an Army nurse. *Hospital Sketches*, written at that time was my first published work.

No matter what else demanded my time, there were two things I did every day. One was to write. Something. Anything. But every day I wrote. The second was to run in the woods. I had done this from my earliest childhood and continued to do so as long as my body allowed.

When I was thirty-seven the first section of *Little Women* was published, with part two appearing the following year. From that moment on we never again suffered financial problems. I was able to provide a comfortable life for my beloved family.

So, that is my story. What has this to do with my Credo, my statement of personal beliefs? I know that I was a Unitarian, though not necessarily the "churchy" kind. Like my father and William Ellery Channing, I believed deeply that every human being was made in "the image of God." Just as our family's dearest friend, Waldo Emerson, believed, I felt that God was not to be found in creeds, dogmas, or miracles, but rather in the deepest recesses of the human heart. Through Henry David Thoreau, who often took me with him on long walks in the woods, I found divinity in nature.

I once wrote in my journal of an early morning run in the woods. The dew was on the grass; the moss was like velvet; and, as I ran under the arches of yellow and red leaves, I sang for joy, my heart was so light and the world so beautiful. It seemed like going through a dark life or grave into heaven beyond. A very strange and solemn feeling came over me as I stood there, with no sound but the rustle of the pines, no one near me, and the sun so glorious, as if for me alone. I seemed to feel God, as I never had before. I prayed that I might keep that happy sense of nearness all of my life.

Good morning. I am
Olympia Brown

As best I know I was the first woman to be officially ordained to the ministry by any denomination. To be sure there had been women before me who preached, but I was the first to be ordained.

As a student at Mt. Holyoke School for Women I was shocked and dismayed by the forty rules given us to follow, several of which included cautions and admonitions about God's wrath and punishment. I had been raised in a family of Universalists who believed that God was infinitely loving and forgiving. The authorities scoffed at my beliefs and took delight in suggesting I was placing myself in jeopardy of even more severe divine retribution.

I withstood it for one year, and then transferred to Antioch College in Ohio, which had been founded by the Unitarian educational reformer, Horace Mann, just a few years earlier. The atmosphere for me was much more pleasant at Antioch, but I still received no encouragement when I indicated my wish to become a minister. The Unitarians had by that time "recognized" a small number of women who were permitted to preach, but had never granted ordination to a woman.

I agitated on the Antioch campus to have Antoinette Brown invited to speak. Nettie, as she was known, was one of those unordained preachers, an ardent worker for women's rights, and a true heroine of mine. We are not related. When she spoke in the Antioch chapel she set my heart on fire. It was the first time I had ever heard a women preach. A sense of victory lifted my spirits and

I felt high in the air.

I eagerly told her of my desire to be a preacher, too, and she shared her secret – which I believe she shared with you not long ago. Remember her telling you of the white ribbon she wore beneath her collar as a reminder of her dream? Well, she gave me a white ribbon. And I am still wearing it. See?

After college I attended seminary at St. Lawrence, and miracle of miracles, was ordained by the Universalist Church. But that is not the end of my story. My real battles, in fact, were only beginning. Finding a place to preach was the challenge. My first attempt was in a small town in upstate New York, where I simply arrived, announced my intention of preaching and recruited a choir.

My first permanent parish, "settlement" we called it, was in Weymouth, Massachusetts. The church was almost lifeless when I arrived. But the remaining handful of worshipers were loving and supportive and, looking back, I think this may have been my most pleasant pastorate.

It was during this time, the late 1860's, that I became very active in the woman's rights movement and helped organize the New England Woman Suffrage Association.

My second pastorate was in Bridgeport, Connecticut where a small group that had always been opposed to a woman in the pulpit caused a split in the congregation, and I chose to resign rather than seeing the rift becomes permanent.

I then went on to another small, struggling parish in Racine, Wisconsin, in a run-down and unfortunate condition. The pulpits of the prosperous churches were occupied by men, and were the ambition of all the young men coming into the ministry, against whom I had to compete. All I could do was to take a place that had been abandoned by others and make something of it. This I was glad to do.

The church in Racine prospered, and I assumed a growing role in activities of the Wisconsin statewide Suffrage association.

Later I resigned my pulpit and began to work full-time for the suffragist cause. I traveled extensively as a speaker and an organizer campaigning throughout the upper mid-west.

Women who marched in the Suffragist parades always wore white sashes. I remembered the white ribbon Nettie had given me a generation earlier and began to encourage suffragists to wear one when they went campaigning door to door.

I was eighty-five years old when women finally got the vote in 1920. When I walked to the ballot box I was wearing my white ribbon.

I understand that most denominations are ordaining women these days, and that our numbers are continually growing. But I wonder if it is any easier for a woman to find a congregation to minister to now than it was in my pioneering days. How many are still being forced to take whatever is left after the men have made their choice? This may be something you will want to look into, and keep an eye on.

Good morning. I am
Jenkin Lloyd Jones

I was born in 1843 in Cardiganshire County on the west coast of Wales, but was only one year old when our family migrated to America. We settled on a homestead in Wisconsin Territory, about forty miles west of Milwaukee.

My parents, Richard and Mary Lloyd Jones, were Unitarian, a movement, which had been established in Wales in 1795. My guess is that we were the only Unitarians on the Wisconsin frontier.

In my 19th year I was drafted into the Union Army. I served for three years, fought in eleven major battles, and received wounds which caused me to limp for the rest of my life. During those years, I kept a daily journal which chronicled the horrors of war and the unspeakable things war does to people, victors and vanquished alike.

When the war ended I was determined to do something worthwhile with my life, took the $100 of my army pay which I had saved, and enrolled in Meadville Theological School in Pennsylvania to study for the Unitarian ministry. I waited tables, sawed wood, washed windows and worked as a janitor in the dormitory for my board and room. Also, while in Meadville, I fell in love with Susan Baker, a secretary to one of the professors. We married the day after my graduation – and spent our honeymoon at the Western Unitarian Conference in Cleveland.

The Western Conference, comprised of Unitarian Societies in the mid-west and beyond, was in a mini-revolt against the more conservative New England Unitarians. The Boston-centered group had earlier emerged from the liberal wing of the Congregational

Church, but now were unwilling to go further. They sought to establish a theological test of belief in a personal God and allegiance to Jesus. Those of us who were called radicals felt that the imposition of any credal statement defining terms of membership would be the death of liberal religion in America. We held that ethical principles, not theology, were central in religion.

While this controversy raged, I served congregations, first in Winnetka, Illinois and then in Janesville, Wisconsin. In addition to my local pastoral chores, I served as Secretary for the Western Unitarian Conference, founded and edited *Unity*, a liberal publication, and developed a Sunday School curriculum which was based on practical ethical living, rather than memorizing Bible verses and singing jingle songs. The more liberal societies of the west adopted this curriculum, and for a period of time the Western Unitarian Conference virtually became a separate denomination from the East Coast – centered American Unitarian Association. The breach, of course, was eventually closed. But, you know, as painful as that struggle was for persons on both sides of the divide, I hope that Unitarians never stop experiencing internal conflict. Something essential to the unfettered search for truth would be tragically lost if uniformity of thought ever descended on this movement.

In 1882, that would have been when I was thirty-nine, I confided to my wife that I had long hoped to be called to a church in Chicago, and was disappointed that no call had ever come. She said that if that were the case, we ought to move to Chicago and start our own congregation. That is exactly what we did.

I hired a hall over a store on Cottage Grove Avenue on Chicago's south side and nailed a placard to the door announcing that I would be preaching the following Sunday. Twelve people showed up, nine adults and three children. The second Sunday there were thirty-three, and on the third Sunday we doubled to sixty-six. The Church of All Souls was on its way.

I spent the rest of my life with that congregation, and it grew to be one of the most active in Chicago. We maintained living quarters upstairs in the church. The guest room was occupied by my nephew, the architect Frank Lloyd Wright, while he was serving his apprenticeship with a local firm.

When Chicago began planning for the World Columbian exposition in 1893, I suggested that, in addition to celebrating the great economic and material progress which mankind had made since Columbus had landed in the Western Hemisphere, we ought also to celebrate the religious aspects of our common life. This led to my chairmanship of the World Parliament of Religions. That Parliament bought together representatives of all the world religions. It was the most inclusive religious assemblage ever convened. Nothing like it had happened before, and I doubt any thing like it has happened since.

Most of my remaining life was dedicated to the quest for peace. In 1897 when preparations were underway for war with Spain, I spoke out strongly against American imperialism and suggested that the purchase of Spanish possessions would be far less costly and much more honorable than war.

Similarly, I opposed American entry into the World War. So much so, in fact, that my newspaper, *Unity*, was banned from the U.S mails. A fitting validation of my life!

Good morning. I am
Clarence Darrow

Let me tell you a little something about my background. Shortly after my parents, Emily Eddy and Amirus Darrow, were married in Amboy, Ohio in 1845 they moved to Meadville, Pennsylvania where my father studied at the Unitarian Seminary. This was the golden age of Unitarianism. Its leaders emphasized learning, literature and rational religion. They promoted peace societies, headed movements for prison reform, advocated the abolition of slavery and helped the poor. Father studied the philosophies of such thinkers as William Emery Channing, Ralph Waldo Emerson and Theodore Parker. My parents were so impressed with the Unitarian abolitionist Edward Everett they named their firstborn son, Everett, after him.

Father became a Unitarian minister and before long even the mild tenets of that church could not contain him. Even before I was born, in 1857, he had renounced the church completely, resigned his ministry and become a combination furniture maker and town undertaker.

He remained a dreamer. He was always involved in one or more unpopular causes to which he gave his undivided attention to the neglect of his work. I often thought that had he lost his idealism along with his religion he would have been considerably more prosperous.

But that was the legacy he left to me: Religious doubt and an affinity for unpopular causes. Fortunately, from my mother's side of the family, I also inherited a more Protestant work ethic.

My chosen field, of course, was law. I was a practicing attorney in Chicago from 1878 until the mid 1930s. I was counsel for Eugene Debs, the Socialist leader indicted for conspiracy in the Railroad Union case. I was defense counsel for Nathan Leopold and Richard Loeb. I defended John Scopes in Tennessee when he was prosecuted for teaching evolution in the public schools. I was lawyer to the African American defendants in the infamous Scottsboro case in Alabama. It is fair to say, in fact, that for more than four decades there was not a high profile human rights or civil liberties case in this country in which I was not involved to some degree.

But through it all, I never joined a church. I had many warm and devoted friends of all faiths and of no faith. Two Catholic priests, Father Barett of Lowell and Father Brummer in Chicago, were particularly close. I often quoted them in conversation. Once, when a woman eavesdropper on a train interrupted and asked, "Mr. Darrow, are you a Catholic?" I told her, "No, but if I were going to belong to any church it would be the Catholic Church. Just as I were buying life insurance, I would buy it in a mutual company and not a stock company."

Stories constantly circulated that I had joined one church or another. Since I was recognized as America's most outspoken atheist, religious folk seemed to take special delight in announcing my conversion here or there.

It was once reported that while in a hospital in Denver I had called for an Episcopal bishop and asked to be saved. The truth is that I was, indeed, visited in a Denver hospital by an Episcopal bishop, a nice fellow, by the name of Johnson. I was not really sick. I had just checked in for a few days rest. The Bishop and I had a nice talk, but I don't recall that religion came up in the conversation. I could never put that rumor to rest. It followed me for the remainder of my days.

Another time a reporter in St. Paul relayed to me information about a Humanist Society in Minneapolis which was purely agnostic and anthropocentric, transferring man's loyalty and obligation from God to man. He asked me if I could join such a society. I answered that if it was, indeed, purely humanistic as he had described that I would have no intellectual difficulty in being part of it.

The next day banner headlines across the country announced: DARROW JOINS RELIGIOUS SOCIETY. The Humanist Society in Minneapolis, it seems, was an adjunct of the Unitarian Church, so the press release said, "It was confirmed today that Clarence Darrow, long known as America's leading agnostic, has become a church member."

John Dietrich, minister of the Unitarian Church in the city, was most gracious. He did everything in his power to correct the misrepresentation. Nonetheless newspapers continued for years to report that "Darrow got scared and joined the church."

I am also aware that some Unitarian publications, to this day, still claim me as a member. I guess I should be flattered you would want me.

Thanks for giving me the opportunity to set the record straight. The defense rests.

Good morning. I am
William Howard Taft

I was the sixth Unitarian elected to the presidency of the United States. Those preceding me in the office were John Adams, Thomas Jefferson, John Quincy Adams, Millard Fillmore and Chester Arthur.

You may know that I also was at various time a lawyer in Cincinnati, judge of the Superior Court of Ohio, Solicitor General of the United States, the first civil governor of the Philippines, Secretary of War, and Chief Justice of the United States. You may not know that in the years between my presidency and my appointment to the Supreme Court, I served as president of the Unitarian General Conference.

Unitarianism was an important part of my life. Let me give you two illustrations.

From the time I was eight until I was fifteen my father was a judge of the Superior Court. A Catholic group petitioned the Cincinnati school board to ban the use of the King James, i.e. Protestant, Bible in public school classrooms. A Protestant group filed suit to prohibit the board from acting on this request. You understand, of course, that in Ohio in those days most Protestants were Republicans and most Catholics were Democrats. Two of the three judges hearing the case ruled that the Board could not end religious instruction or prohibit the use of the Protestant Bible.

My father, both Republican and Unitarian, felt the law was clearly on the side of separation of Church and State. He filed a dissenting minority opinion. The Ohio Supreme Court subsequently upheld his view and overturned the majority ruling.

Our entire family was attacked as ungodly, immoral, atheistic. Father was accused of being a traitor both to the Republican Party and to his "social class."

It mattered little that the Tafts were faithful churchgoers, seldom missing a service at our Unitarian Church. The protesting Protestants never forgave him. His promising political career was severely damaged. Still, he told me many times that he never regretted his decision and considered it one of the most important of his judicial career.

Forty years later in 1899, the Yale Corporation offered me the presidency of Yale, my alma mater. I refused their offer, primarily because of my religious affiliation. "Yale's strongest support," I reminded them, "comes from among those who believe in the creed of the orthodox, evangelical churches. I am a Unitarian. I believe in God. I do not believe in the divinity of Christ and there are many other postulates of the orthodox creed to which I cannot subscribe. The election to the presidency of the University of such a one would shock the large conservative element of those who give Yale her power and influence in the country." Fortunately for me my political opponents never got hold of that private letter. If they had I can assure you that William Jennings Bryan, rather that William Howard Taft would have been elected the 27th president of the United States.

My term as president of the General Conference coincided with the period of ascendancy of the Social Gospel. This put me in conflict with many of my fellow Unitarians. My own conservative convictions, earnestly arrived at through vigorous self-searching, were very different from those held by persons such as the Reverent Dr. John Haynes Holmes of New York's Church of the Messiah.

In 1908, the same year I was elected president of the United States, Holmes had been the leading figure in the creation of the Unitarian Fellowship for Social Justice. This agency reflected the view of many who, like Holmes, were Socialists and pacifists and strong supporters of organized labor.

At the General Assembly in 1917 a resolution was passed

supporting President Wilson and the American war effort. Holmes and his followers sought to add a rider to the resolution indicating there was strong minority objection to it. I left the chair as presiding officer and spoke vigorously in opposition to the addition. The assembly sided with me.

I may have been right on these issues, or I may have been wrong. Who is to say for certain?

What is important, it seems to me, is that the fundamental Unitarian tenet of freedom of thought and freedom of speech was not compromised.

If my experience teaches nothing else, it at least proves one does not have to be politically liberal to be a Unitarian.

Good morning. I am
Jane Addams

For nearly fifty years, from 1889 to 1935, I was the director of Hull House on Halstead Street in Chicago. This Settlement House, as it was called, was the fulfillment of a childhood dream – though it took me quite a while to make the connection.

I was born in Western Illinois in 1860 the year Abraham Lincoln was elected president. My father was the wealthiest man in our village of Cedarville and in nearby Freeport. He owned a flourmill, a sawmill, was president of the local bank and a respected member of the State Senate.

He was a longtime friend of Lincoln, and a leading member among the group of state politicians which organized the Republican Party. One of my cherished possessions was a portfolio of letters Lincoln wrote to Father; all addressed "Dear Double-D Addams" in reference to the rather unusual spelling of our last name.

My mother died in childbirth two years after I was born and father did not remarry until I was ten, so he was my anchor in early life. Once when I was eight or nine, he took me with him in our horse drawn carriage to a section of Freeport I had never seen before. The houses were small and crowded and dilapidated. I was shocked, not having seen such poverty before. I suppose I had assumed that everyone enjoyed the kind of luxurious comfort with which we were blessed. One the way home, I told my father, "When I grow up I want to live in a big house, but I want it to be close to the houses where the poor people live so that I can invite them to visit me."

Then, for all practical purposes I forgot about my vision for two decades. I grew up and attended Rockford Seminary, then enrolled in the Woman's Medical School in Philadelphia. I completed one year of medical studies before health problems forced me to leave school and return home. I had been born with curvature of the spine. In Philadelphia this problem worsened and an operation became necessary. I required more than six months of bed rest to recover. My doctor counseled me to forget my idea of becoming a physician and recommended instead that I take my rather sizeable inheritance and travel in Europe.

For several years, I traveled back and forth across the Atlantic numerous times. But I was not happy. I once wrote in my journal, "I am tired of living and would gladly choose death, except that I believe it cowardly to die before one has done something worthwhile."

I found that "something worthwhile" at Toynbee Hall, a Settlement House founded by an English clergyman in London's miserable East End. I remembered what I had once told my father.

In 1888 I returned to America, moved to Chicago and began my search for the big house near the little houses. I found it right in the middle of the tenements on Halstead Street, the very center of Chicago's foreign immigrant quarter.

Gracious old Hull House, built forty years earlier, had been abandoned by the Hull family when immigrants began to arrive. It now stood nearly empty, used only as a factory storehouse. It was perfect for my needs! If found the owners, explained what I intended for the house, and they deeded it to me free of charge – happy to no longer have to pay the taxes.

I spent my own money renovating and redecorating the house. It was not my intention to live in poverty. Rather, it was my intention to help them rise out of poverty and live in the comfort that I enjoyed. If that seems strange to you, I can only say that is truthful testimony of my intent. I was not a martyr or a saint. I created a place of beauty and invited others to sample it. We provided day care for working mothers, a medical clinic for those who were denied access to private physicians, recreation programs for young people, pre-school education for children, job resource center – whatever the need we sought to provide relief.

Mostly we strove to promote the Kingdom of God on earth by improving working conditions, building better housing and sewerage systems, getting pure water and sanitary facilities, parks and playgrounds – eventually eliminating poverty.

Toward that end, for seven years I personally rose at 6:00 a.m. every weekday and followed the city garbage wagon through our neighborhood making sure it did the job it was supposed to do.

Yes, in the beginning we did believe that we were engaged in a Christian missionary enterprise. But we never held religious services at the House. That would not have been appropriate for the people we were seeking to serve.

During those years, when I went to church at all, it was to the Unitarian All Souls Church where Jenkin Lloyd Jones was the prophetic leader. I guess that makes me a Unitarian though I don't believe I ever officially joined. Later in my life I became a convinced agnostic, but that didn't seem to bother the Unitarians who were pretty much the same. Giving other human beings the opportunity to enrich and elevate themselves was what Hull House was about. And, that is enough for me.

Good morning. I am
Charles Proteus Steinmetz

Actually, when I was born in Breslau, Germany in 1865 I was christened Karl August Rudolph Steinmetz. It was only after I migrated to America that I anglicized my name from Karl to Charles and exchanged August Rudolph for a college nickname Proteus.

My father worked for the railroad and he dreamed that I might have the kind of mechanical aptitude which would permit me to follow him in this occupation. When I was quite young he bought me a toy locomotive, equipped with piston and driving wheels and which used alcohol for fuel. I kept that toy train throughout my entire life.

We were nominally Lutherans, and I was confirmed at age thirteen, though I must confess it meant very little to me at the time, and later even less.

I studied at the University of Breslau. I had always had a strong interest in mathematics and developed a fascination with electricity, which was becoming a subject of academic study.

I was a dedicated student, never missing a lecture, which was exceedingly unusual at European Universities at that time. In your day I would surely be termed a "grind."

In addition to my studies I also became active in the Socialist Club. These were the days of Bismarck in Germany, and our activities (though quite benign, idealistic and utopian) were watched carefully by the police. In fact, two weeks before my doctorial degree was to be conferred, I was forced to flee to

Switzerland to keep from being imprisoned for sedition.

A year later I was able to migrate to America where I began my career as an electrical engineer. I specialized in research related to magnetism and alternating current. I will not bore you with technical details of my scientific work. Suffice is to say that every time you use an electrical appliance you benefit from my work in the General Electric Laboratories.

Through the influence of Joseph Hayden, my foster-son and young protégé, I became associated with Rev. Ernest Caldecott and his ministry, All Souls Unitarian Church in Schenectady, New York. I was not a regular churchgoer, but never missed on those occasions when children were on the program.

Since I was asked, specifically, to share with you my views on religion, I will quote directly from a speech I delivered in 1922 at the All Souls Church. My subject was "The Place of Religion in Modern Scientific Civilization."

"Religion may be defined as dealing with the relations of man to superior entities, usually conceived as a personal God or personal Gods. Science as understood here, deals with the conclusions derived by the laws of logic from our observations of the physical world.

"There has grown up through the centuries an increasing antagonism between science and religion. Religion met this by the Inquisition, that is, by forcibly suppressing science and its votaries.

"However, our civilization is an engineering civilization. Engineering is the application of science to the service of mankind, and thus the dominating factor in our human society.

"Therefore in civilized countries, any attempt by religion to suppress science as was done in medieval times is laughed out of court. The attempts, for example, to use legislation to forbid the teaching of evolution is rarely successful; at least, not for a very long period of time.

"In the realm of science, all attempts to find any evidence of supernatural beings, of metaphysical conceptions, such as God, have failed. If we are honest we must confess that in science God does not exist.

84

"But this really means nothing except that we cannot get by reasoning a conclusion which is not contained in the premises on which we started our reasoning. Thus the negative answer of science about the existence of God is not conclusive. The question is still as open as ever.

"The foundation of religion is belief and faith. Science is based on logical reasoning from facts. These are two different things. Science and religion are not antagonistic. They are simple separate. One deals with finite conclusions from the world of facts, and the other with infinite conceptions which can neither be proved or disproved empirically, but are outside the realm of science, in the realm of faith.

"A collision between science and religion can only occur when the one tries to encroach on the field of the other, as, for instance, when religion attempts to teach history in the fable of the creation of the world, or biology in opposing the theory of evolution. These are not proper and essential parts of religion. They are mere survivors of the pre-scientific age of man's history."

Good morning. I am
Frank Lloyd Wright

A third generation birthright Unitarian.

Back in Wales, in the Victorian Era, there lived a hatter who made strange, black, high pointed cones. Witches wore them while riding on their brooms. The Welsh wore them simply as hats.

On Sundays the hat maker preached; a firebrand of a man, questioning how man should be just with God, rejecting the answers most men, and women too, gave him.

This was Richard Jones, tall, dark-eyed, an impassioned unpopular Unitarian. May Lloyd, the daughter of an old Welsh family heard him, fell in love with him, and went away with him against her family's will. They had seven children, who bore the family names Lloyd-Jones.

In his fifty-third year the hatter-preacher immigrated with his delicate wife and seven offspring to Wisconsin, believing the American frontier would provide more hospitable environs for his outspoken liberality.

Among those seven children were Jenkin Lloyd Jones, who grew up to be one of America's most renowned and highly respected Unitarian ministers, and my mother Anna.

Anna was devoted to education and to teaching. She did not marry until she was twenty-nine, when she at last found a man who satisfied her notions of education. He was William Russell Wright, a musician from Connecticut, now a circuit rider teaching voice to people on the frontier.

He had first studied medicine before choosing music, and was now hearing a call to preach. Anna helped him hear that call. Soon after they were married he, too, became a Unitarian minister.

Soon Anna had a son. A son who, she said, would build great and beautiful buildings. Before he was born, she would say, she intended him to be an architect.

As a young boy I lay in bed at night listening intently to my father playing Bach, Beethoven and Mozart on the parlor piano. I could analyze the mathematical structure of those compositions and translate them in my mind into physical edifices. If Bach had not chosen music he would have been a great architect, just as I feel I would have been a great musician if mother had not preordained me to be an architect.

I walked the Wisconsin woods, observing the trees on the ridge of surrounding hills. I saw them standing like various buildings, of more different kinds than all the architectures of the world. Someday I learned that the secret of all styles in architecture was the same secret that gave character to the trees. And I knew that Truth could only be discovered when structure was permitted to emerge from its organic environment. Against the counsel of both my mother and my Uncle Jenkin I left college before graduation and moved to Chicago to apprentice under Louis Sullivan. There I lived in the parsonage of my uncle's All Souls Church.

Shortly after arriving in Chicago my mother wrote me: "I would have you a man of sense as well as sensibility. You will find Goodness and Truth everywhere you go. If you have to choose, choose Truth. For that is the closest to Earth, my boy: in that lies strength. Simplicity of heart is just as necessary for an architect as for a farmer or a minister if the architect is to build great buildings."

I always tried to follow her advice, even though adherence to Truth, as I understood it, brought with it hardship and conflict.

The interconnected relationship between my religious heritage and my profession can best be illustrated, I believe, by telling you about the creation and construction of Unity Church for the Universalist congregation in Oak Park, Illinois.

The building committee had in mind a little white New England style church with a lean spire pointing to heaven. That was the only style they knew.

I told them a story. Did they not know the tale of the holy man who, yearning to see God, climbed up and up to the highest mountain? There, ragged and worn, he lifted up his eager perspiring face to heaven and called upon God. He heard a voice bidding him get down – Go back!

Would he really see God's face? Then he should go back down, down to the valley below where his own people were – there, only, could he look upon God's countenance.

Why not, then, build a temple, not with a steeple pointing up to God – more sentimental than sensible – but build a temple to man, appropriate to his uses as a meetinghouse, in which to study himself for God's sake?

Ponder that and you will discover what I believe.

Good morning, I am
Edgar Ethelred Brown

I was minister of the Harlem Unitarian Church from 1920 to 1956. I was born and raised in Jamaica and followed my father into Civil Service. I am told that as a child I was unusually inquisitive and unfailingly honest. I am not able to judge whether those impressions of my nature were true, but have no reason to question the validity of the observations of those who knew me, and loved me, best.

I do know that my inquisitiveness and honesty led me into difficulties with the orthodox religious teachings of my church, at a very early age. I think I had hardly learned to count as far as three when I began to have difficulty with the strangeness of the Trinitarian arithmetic, as recited in the Creed of our family church.

Several years later I fortuitously came upon a copy of Channing's *Unitarian Christianity*, and knew that I had found an answer to my intellectual dilemma. I remained a loyal member of my church, serving for a number of years as organist and choir director. But in my mind, and in my heart, I knew I was a Unitarian without a church.

In 1907, when I was thirty-two years of age, I lost my Civil Service position. But, rather than despairing at this unfortunate circumstance, I took it as an unquestionable sign that I was being called to become a minister.

This had been in the back of my mind for at least a decade, but it took dismissal from what I had assumed was a protected, life long position to give me the stimulus and courage to pursue my dream.

The African Methodist Church in Jamaica hailed my decision and was prepared to welcome me with open arms, but this was not the direction I wished to take.

I wrote a letter to Meadville Theological School, explaining my circumstances and my desire to become a Unitarian minister. President Franklin Southworth's reply was frank and not encouraging. He told me that there was no Unitarian Church in America for colored people, and since white Unitarians required a white minister he was unable to predict what my future would hold at the conclusion of my training. But, at the same time, he did inform me that I would be accepted at the Seminary as long as I accepted the uncertainty of my future.

If President Southworth thought that would discourage me from coming to America, it was because he did not yet know me very well. I knew that I wanted to be a minister, but only in a church where I could be completely honest. So, I appreciated the fact that he had been completely honest with me even when the answer was less than I would have wished to hear.

It took me more than a year to solve some financial problems and with my immigration status, before I could begin a special two-year course at Meadville.

I went home to Jamaica convinced I could establish a Unitarian presence on my native soil. After a decade of fruitless effort, I forwent that experiment and moved to New York to organize a Unitarian Church in Harlem.

I started with no members and no place to meet and, for the first ten or eleven years, no help from the American Unitarian Association. I arranged for meeting space at the West Indian Association Lodge Room, and later as the congregation began to grow, at the Harlem YWCA. John Haynes Holmes, minister of the New York Community Church took an interest in me and in our work and provided great help during our years of struggle.

After Frederick May Eliot assumed leadership of the Unitarian Association in the mid-1930s our work was recognized and the congregation was accepted into the larger organization. We had called ourselves a Unitarian Church for seventeen years before the

Unitarians agreed to accept us.

Even then the relationship remained rocky, and I am frank to admit that a part of the fault was my own stubbornness. We had our way of seeing things and doing things, and the white leadership of the denomination had their ways. The two tracks did not always run parallel.

They thought that I, and my congregation, were too deeply involved in political affairs. I said that people of color had to be involved in the political arena. It was not only a religious imperative, but also a condition of survival. It is not surprising they could not quite grasp that situation.

I wish I could tell you that I developed a large and thriving congregation during the thirty-six years I served as minister, but that would not be true. We never truly achieved financial stability. But our work did not fail. We leavened Harlem. We compelled many other churches to soften the emphasis on old outmoded doctrines – and Harlem is a better place because we were there.

Some said I was too impractical, too much of an idealist and a dreamer. I contend that those who visualize better days and believe that visions can come true are the truly practical people.

Throughout it all I never lost faith. I never regretted my decision to cast my lot with the Unitarians even when they were not sure they wanted me. No. No. That is not true. I am sure that they always wanted me. It was just that they did not know it at the time.

Good morning. I am
Albert Schweitzer

I was born in 1875 in the little village of Kayserberg in Alsace, which at that time was part of Germany. When I was yet an infant my father, a Lutheran pastor, was called to minister in Gunsbach. It was there I grew up.

As a boy my first love was music. I was, I suppose, what would be called a child prodigy. When I was only eight, with legs that would barely touch the pedals, I began to play the organ for services in the Gunsbach church.

By my late teens I was dividing my time between the University of Strasbourg where I was studying theology, and Paris where the famous organist and composer Charles Marie Widor had taken me on as a student and protégé.

That should have been sufficient, but I felt a sense of emptiness – a sense that I should be doing more for the suffering humanity of the world. I made a vow to myself at age twenty-one that I would continue with theology and music until I was thirty. All my years after that would be devoted to the service of my fellow man, though I did not yet know at that time what form or direction that service might take.

I accepted the responsibilities of preaching and teaching at St. Nicholas Church in Strasbourg and began to perform organ concerts in Paris and elsewhere. One day I picked up a magazine published by The Paris Missionary Society and read an article entitled "The Needs of the Congo Mission." By the time I finished reading that article the course of my future life was determined. I would go to French Equatorial Africa and practice medicine there.

I enrolled in medical school and spent the next three years studying, making a specialty in tropical diseases. On Easter Sunday, 1913, I played the great organ at St. Sulpice for the last time. When I finished, the Paris Bach Society presented me with a piano fitted with organ pedals. Packed in a lead-lined case to withstand the tropical climate of Africa, their gracious gift accompanied my bride, Helen, and me to Lambarene, located in what is now Gabon.

With only minor interruptions this was where I remained for the next six decades. We found nothing more than a chicken coop for both home and hospital when we first arrived, but we felt we had landed in the Garden of Eden. I was Oganga, the healer, and I knew this was who I had been destined to become.

I'll not weary you this morning with details of my theology. I have gone to great lengths in several books if this is your interest. Suffice is to say that as a scientist I applied scientific methods to my studies and gave little credence to metaphysical or transcendental ideas.

The core of my faith is summed up in the phrase: Reverence for Life. I had long struggled with the problem of man's cruelty to his fellow man. Then one day I observed four hippopotami and their young on a sandbank of a river. Seeing how these huge yet humble hippos cared for their young was my answer. The reason people were so cruel to one another was because they did not care. Only by nurturing reverence for life could we learn to treat others – and all living creatures – as we ought. That simple insight became my key to unlocking the mystery of life.

Now let me say a few words about my relationship with the Unitarians. Even as a theological student I had great admiration for the early Unitarians and their affirmation of religious freedom even when it meant persecution. Also, there was much in the way we addressed matters such as the Trinity and the divinity of Jesus that drew us close.

Once, in the immediate aftermath of World War II, my hospital was heavily in debt and threatened with closure. At that very moment Dr. Charles Joy, of the Unitarian Service Committee in America, and Mr. Melvin Arnold, the editor-in-chief of your *Beacon Press*, arrived in Lambarene with a check which more than covered our indebtedness and allowed our hospital to continue. In subsequent years Melvin Arnold probably did more than anyone else to make my work known as widely in America as it was in Europe. So my respect and gratitude to the Unitarians was warm and well placed.

Then in 1961, which was my 86th year, I received a letter from George Marshall, the minister of the Church of the Larger Fellowship (Unitarian Universalist) in Boston, asking if I would accept honorary membership in his congregation.

I wrote back immediately, thanking him for the honor. My letter was reprinted in the Newsletter for Religious Liberals, and many people thought I had rejected my life-long Lutheranism to be a Unitarian. A minor uproar erupted on both sides of the Atlantic. Finally, I had to clarify the matter by telling Time Magazine that while my relations with the Unitarians were meaningful and strong I had not made a break with the Lutheran Church.

So, I leave it to you to decide whether I ever was a Unitarian. I'm happy either way.

Good morning. I am
John Haynes Holmes

On the first Sunday in February 1907, at age twenty-seven, I preached my first sermon at the Unitarian Church of the Messiah on Park Avenue in New York City. My topic was "The Church and The New Age." We were in a new century. Progress seemed inevitable. I was calling for a church, which could measure up to the promise of the times. "Every man will be an authority unto himself," I said. "The tyranny of creeds will be abolished and each man will chant the credo written on the tablet of his soul. We will usher in an era of good feeling, the end of bitterness, strife, bigotry and ill will."

On the very same day, less than a mile away, Rabbi Stephen Wise developed nearly the same theme at his newly organized Free Synagogue. Shortly thereafter we met, compared notes, and began a friendship and cooperative relationship which lasted more than half a century, and through many many battles on behalf of an enlightened humanity. The reality of my friendship with Rabbi Wise is, I believe, at the heart of any creed I might profess.

I was the product of New England Puritan stock. The Holmes family had been in America for nearly two centuries before my businessman grandfather heeded the appeal of Ellery Channing and Theodore Parker to move beyond established Congregationalism and become Unitarian. In fact, my grandfather was one of the men who determined that the radical Parker should have a place to preach and arranged for the use of the Melodeon ballroom in 1845.

My early decision to study at Harvard and enter the Unitarian ministry was a very natural, almost predetermined, one. But I was also prepared to move beyond the Unitarianism of my day. The purpose of religion, as I saw it, was not so much to redeem the individual as to redeem society. To do this the church had to be totally immersed in the world of politics, economics and social policy.

Politically I was a Socialist. The Capitalist system, based on competition and greed, could never serve the common good. If there were winners there had to be losers, and the ever-growing disparity between the rich and the poor was a violation of every value I held dear. From my pulpit I supported Eugene Debs, Norman Thomas, Robert LaFollette, without apology or regret.

With regard to war I was a pacifist. I was founding member of the Fellowship of Reconciliation. I opposed our entry into the World War, ignoring the rabid nationalistic hysteria which swept the country at that time. To me it was a simple question. If war was right then Christianity was wrong, false, a lie. If Christianity is right, then war is wrong, false, a lie.

I was warned by many, at the time, that preaching such things would destroy the church. Surprisingly, our membership actually increased during that period.

The 1917 meeting of the General Conference had resolutions before it calling for full support of America's war effort. I submitted a substitute resolution, which asked that a minority view, in opposition to all war, be attached to the majority opinion. Under blistering attack from former President William Howard Taft, who was chairing the session, I was voted down 236-9. I had been considering my future relationship with the Unitarian Association for some time, and that resounding defeat encouraged further consideration.

A year later, I proposed to my congregation that we withdraw from the Association and become a Community Church. It was to be a place for a universal, humanistic religion, free of every vestige of theology, relegating matters of belief to private individual opinion, and welcoming to our church any person, rich or poor, black or white, Christian, Jew, Muslim, Hindu. Parsee.

I would hope that this definition is so ordinary as to sound trite in your generation. In 1920 it was a revolutionary notion, even for Unitarians.

We became the Community Church of New York, and I continued as its minister until I retired in 1949.

Over the years, I was involved in the organization of the National Association for the Advancement of Colored People, the American Civil Liberties Union and the American Christian Palestine Committee.

I have been credited with having introduced Mohandas Gandhi to the American public. In 1920 I preached a sermon entitled "Who Is The Greatest Man In The World Today?" To almost everyone's surprise I said it was Gandhi, then relatively unknown to the American public. I said at the time "if I believed in the Second Coming – which I do not – I should dare assert that Gandhi was Jesus come back to earth."

So I lived my life. A Puritan without Calvinist theology, convinced that progress is still possible, that God moves in both nature and history, and we were created for destinies higher than those of this earth alone.

Good morning. I am
Clarence Russell Skinner

As a student at St. Lawrence College in Canton, NY at the turn of the 20th century, I had decisions to make. One was easy: to marry Clara, a beautiful student who was also the organist at the local Universalist Church. Another was more difficult: to choose whether to go into the ministry or to pursue a career in the theater.

Both of these professions figured heavily in my heritage. My father was a playwright and the drama critic for the *Brooklyn Eagle*. His brother, Otis Skinner, was a famous actor. My own brother Harold was on the stage and I had acted in a number of campus plays.

On the other hand, several generations of Skinners had been prominent in Universalist religious and educational affairs. My paternal grandfather and great-grandfather had been Universalist ministers. Otis Ainsworth Skinner, a more distant relative, had established Tufts College in Massachusetts. When Tufts needed additional funds to open the college to women, my grandmother, Cornelia B. Skinner, led the campaign to raise $100,000 from Universalist women and donated her own camel's hair shawl and diamond ring to the cause.

Ultimately, I chose to enter the ministry. There were two prevailing reasons. As a minister I would have the opportunity to pursue causes of human rights and social justice, which were very dear to me. I would have the right to speak my own convictions rather than simply repeating the words others had written for the stage. Also I knew the ministry and would provide a more satisfactory and stable home life.

I was ordained in 1906 and called to the Universalist Church in Mt.Vernon, New York. At approximately the same time John Haynes Holmes came to minister at a Unitarian Church in New York City. We became great friends and collaborators. We both believed that the church had to move beyond its limiting concern of saving the souls of a few within a bad society and strive to create a just society in which all could have a good life. Religion had to be applied to the whole range of human affairs – in education, politics, industry and international relations.

Holmes and I became leaders of this Social Gospel movement in our respective denominations. In 1908 he founded the Unitarian Fellowship for Social Justice and two years later I founded the Universalist Social Service Commission and formulated a Declaration of Social Principles which became the platform for social ethics of the Universalist denomination.

Even though our two denominations – Unitarian and Universalist – were the most liberal of the Protestant groups, our ideas of social responsibilities of the church were met by fierce opposition in many quarters. There were many who held firmly to the belief that religion was a personal matter, a relationship between a person and his or her God – and to be concerned about social justice was nothing more than meddling in politics where religion did not belong. Yes, my friends, early in this century many Universalists and Unitarians felt that way!

I was teaching in the Seminary at Tufts when World War I broke out. I was then, and remained throughout my life, a dedicated pacifist. I believe that war is wrong, that it creates worse problems than it could ever solve, and that universal disarmament was necessary to break the ever recurring cycle of violence.

These were not popular ideas. Unless you lived through the World War I period it will be impossible for you to imagine the anti-Germanic hysteria which gripped America at the time. Anything German was taboo. The German language was forbidden in the schools. German measles were renamed Liberty measles. A man in Buffalo who had a German shepherd named Kaiser was denied a dog license until he changed the name. At my own

99

college, Tufts, the president armed the male students with Indian clubs he had confiscated from the women's gymnasium to be used to repel the enemy in case of a German invasion of our campus.

Needless to say, it was a difficult time for those of us who chose to stand firm in our opposition to war. But, in whatever forum I could find, I continued to call for international cooperation and total disarmament in the postwar period.

In 1919 I organized the Community Church in Boston, to provide a church for those whose religious needs were not being met by any denomination. We started meeting in a small community auditorium and later grew to fill all 2600 seats in Boston's Symphony Hall regularly.

I continued teaching in the Seminary, with an emphasis on Comparative Religions. I discovered so many common threads among all the world's major faiths. I came to fervently believe one's religious pilgrimage must explore many paths. I always attempted to teach about another faith as sympathetically as if it were being taught by an adherent of that faith itself. One of my students once wrote at the bottom of a test paper on Confucianism: "Professor Skinner, almost thou persuadest me to be a heathen." I guess that it is the way I would best like to be remembered.

Good morning. I am
Buckminster Fuller

You may call me Bucky. All my friends do.

The Fuller side of my family was well-known for its long line of intellectuals and rebels – Unitarian ministers, lawyers, writers – from my great grandfather, the Reverend Timothy Fuller who was a delegate to the Massachusetts Constituent Assembly, but opposed the ratification of the Constitution because it did not prohibit slavery; to Timothy, Jr. who graduated second instead of first in his Harvard class of 1801 because he took part in a student rebellion; to my grandfather, an all-out Abolitionist who was killed leading a successful Union attack in Fredericksburg.

I didn't learn about my great-Aunt Margaret Fuller until I was grown. Nobody played up the Fuller's intellectual side. Aunt Margaret was just somebody in the family to me.

When I was a boy, Emerson was celebrated as a poet and essayist. Everyone knew about him. But it wasn't until later that I learned about the extraordinary influence my own Aunt Margaret had on him.

She convinced him he should be published, and together they founded *The Dial*, with Aunt Margaret as editor. This became the "official journal" of the Transcendentalist movement and, under the editorship, Thoreau and others were first published and became known.

She was literary critic for the New York Tribune, the first woman war correspondent, one of the world's leading interpreters of Goethe – but uppermost, the intellectual forerunner of the

Women's Movement that emerged in the middle of the 19th century.

A professor at Oxford once gave me a bit of verse:

Fuller is the name, for better of for worse.

Of two who grappled with the universe.

"I'll accept it," said Margaret the spinster;

"I'll explain it," said bold Buckminster.

Of course she did marry near the end of her short life, but it wouldn't rhyme that way.

Hearing that Aunt Margaret had said, "I must start with the universe and work down to its parts, I must have understanding of it," was a great impetus for me.

I saw that my education was pushing me to be a specialist. Everyone is being led to specialize to a point at which they cannot be synergetic and can only know about the parts instead of the whole. Very deliberately I became a comprehensivist.

My life's work was called Architectural Engineering, but what I was really doing all those years was trying to discover the principles of nature and apply them to new uses.

Very early I said to myself, I'm just an individual. I can't reform the human race, but I may be able to improve on its environment.

I did this by trying to approach things as a child. Children have a deeper reverence for whatever truth and love may be. We'll make it on this planet because of them.

Human beings are born naked, helpless, ignorant, and curious. We now know we have been aboard our planet for about 2 million years, and we've had to grow from being "naked," learning by trial and error, without words to expanding verbal communication capability and vast knowledge.

We are able to explore the universe in ways previous generations could only dream. In that process we have discovered that muscle is nothing and mind is everything.

Evolution is integrating us. We are no longer remote from each other. Clearly we are here to use our minds, to be information gatherers in the local universe, problem solvers in relationship to the maintenance of the integrity of the eternally regenerative universe.

Muscle is nothing; mind is everything. But muscle is still in control of human affairs.

In a few years if we come out with muscle in control, we will have chosen oblivion.

If we come out with mind in control, we will have chosen utopia and eternity.

People often tell me I'm an optimist, and I say, I am a very hard realist. I know we have the option to make it, and that is very different from being an optimist. Yes, we do have the option to make it, but it is absolutely touch and go. It is a matter of integrity of every human being from now on.

Either you are going to go along with your mind and truth or you are going to yield to fear and custom and conditioned reflexes.

With our minds alone we can discover those principles we need to employ to convert all humanity to success in a new, harmonious relationship with the universe.

This is my Credo. That is my challenge to you.

Good morning. I am
Adlai Stevenson

My paternal grandfather, the original Adlai Ewing Stevenson, who served as Vice President during Grover Cleveland's second term, was a Democrat and a Presbyterian. My maternal grandfather, W.O. Davis was a Republican and a Unitarian.

Being a born politician, I found my politics in the Stevenson side of the family and my religion in the Davis side. I became a Democrat and a Unitarian, thus keeping both sides of the family somewhat satisfied.

I remember with fondness the old Unitarian Church in Bloomington, Illinois which I attended faithfully as a boy. I'm sure the Sunday School superintendent, Mr. Pearce, has not yet recovered from his shock and surprise at who I became after leaving his tutelage.

I will not recount for you this morning my political career, or my two unsuccessful campaigns for the presidency. Even now, it still "hurts to much to laugh."

What I will do, with your permission, is repeat some of what I said when delivering the first A. Powell Davis lecture at Constitution Hall in Washington, D.C. in 1959. Davies was the longtime prophetic minister of All Souls Unitarian Church in the nation's capital, and a dear friend of mine for many years.

A central theme of his preaching was that "the world is too dangerous for anything but truth, and too small for anything but brotherhood." I took that as the starting point for my lecture which, in reality, was my Credo.

We Americans have been stifled with complacent self-confidence. We have believed ourselves to be dominant in every field. We have boasted of the American Century. We have forgotten the ardors and efforts that have given us a measure of pre-eminence. The trouble is we have confused the free with the free and easy. The condition of freedom is not only rare today. It has always been rare.

Make no mistake about this. The natural government of man is servitude. Tyranny is the normal pattern. It is only by intense thought, by great effort, by burning idealism and unlimited sacrifice that freedom has prevailed as a system of government. And the efforts which were first necessary to create it are fully as necessary to sustain it in our day.

He who offers this thing we call freedom as the soft option is a deceiver or himself deceived. He who sells it cheap or offers it as a by – product of this or that economic system is a knave or a fool. For freedom demands infinitely more care than any other political system. It puts consent and personal initiative in the place of command and obedience. By thus relying on the devotion of ordinary citizens, it gives up the harsh but effective disciplines that underpin all the tyrannies which over the millennia have stunted the full statute of humankind. I offer three benchmarks to test whether Americans will be capable of regaining the necessary sense of national purpose and the discipline to carry it out.

The first is *remediable poverty*. The affluent society is normal today for a great majority of Americans to a greater or lesser degree. But millions do not share it at all. Poverty can be wiped out, but only if the well-to-do majority of today does not repeat the selfish indifference which has been the epitaph of yesterday's wealthy elite.

Second is the *status of our citizens of color*. If America is to save itself, the civil rights of all citizens must be protected not only by law but by custom. This can never be accomplished unless there are enough white men and women who resist in the core of their beings the moral evil of treating any of God's children as essentially inferior.

The third is *our disproportionate ownership of most of the world's wealth.* The Atlantic world comprises only 16% of the world's peoples, but controls over 80% of the world's wealth. The United States accounts for the lion's share of that. To the moral implications of this gap, we cannot be indifferent. It will require moral insights of justice and compassion to stir us to an understanding of the privileged position which sets us apart from the rest of the world. We are not going to be stirred by our own needs.

I'm counting on you to continue talking sense to the American people.

Good morning. I am
Norman Cousins

You are turning the tables on me this morning. One of the things I am best remembered for was the series of articles I wrote while editor of *The Saturday Review of Literature,* in which I asked a number of prominent world leaders to relate the major lessons they had learned in life.

Asking me to present my Credo is, in essence, the same question – except that I now must answer, rather than ask and report.

I am, as you know, a Unitarian. We Unitarians have many and varied ideas about the existence and/or nature of God. For me God stands in fullest glory not when made to sit astride infinity or when regarded as an architect of cosmic spectacles, but when contemplated as the ultimate force that prevents the cosmic void from being complete.

Whether the Great Design of Creation exists within a microcosm or macrocosm is unimportant; the vital particles have order and purpose and exist. And there is a place inside that order for humanity, for consciousness, for conscience, for love. That is what is important. We are not children of relativity. We are children of God. And, we are brothers and sisters whether we acknowledge that fact or not.

Brotherhood exists, as a fact. What does not exist is the recognition that this is so. Human brotherhood/sisterhood, solidarity – choose your own terminology – is a biological reality. Unfortunately it does not yet serve as the basis for our day-to-day actions or our working philosophies for our behavior as nations. It is oneness without recognition that defines humanity's imperfect knowledge of itself.

The human race may not be tied together politically or philosophically or culturally, but what the world's people do have in common is a finite amount of land, an air envelope that is rapidly filling with filth and poison, and an uneven water supply that is largely unprotected against the infection of sewage and noxious wastes.

The human intelligence that created industrial civilization now must make that civilization compatible with man's basic needs. If this cannot be done, the verdict for the human creature is likely to be that of producer of garbage and poisons, and only secondarily a creator of fine works, great deeds and beauty.

It was that fundamental belief that has motivated me over the years to be a champion of nuclear controls as chairman of the Citizens Committee for a Nuclear Test Ban Treaty; to lead the effort to bring victims of the bombing of Hiroshima to American for medical treatment; to serve as president of the United World Federalists, to editorialize against cigarette advertising, industrial pollution, and violence in the performing arts.

Conservatives thought me a bothersome nag, but I believed that nothing is more powerful than an individual acting out of conscience, thus helping to bring the collective conscience to life.

I was accused to being what Oscar Hammerstein called a "cockeyed optimist." Indeed I was. One of the great losses of the last half-century is the loss of optimism. The belief in human progress and an approximation of the perfectibility of the individual human used to be one of the benchmarks of Unitarianism. What has happened to that?

Optimism is the key to finding a solution to the social problems which confront us, just as optimism is the key to stimulating the healing forces in the body to restore or maintain physical health.

Optimism supplies the basic energy of civilization. Optimism does not wait on facts. It deals with prospects. Pessimism is a waste of time and energy. Progress begins with the idea that progress is possible. Cynicism begins with the notion that retreat and defeat are inevitable.

Many people seem to have grown weary of this struggle for a sane and just society. You must not let that happen to you. Remember you are living life against a backdrop of eternity. Immortality is not a distant and shiny phenomenon but a living reality. You live in others; others have lived in you. So long as any human being lives you have life. Your passport to immortality, to be valid, must have the stamp of the human community on it.

I know what the experts are telling you: that it is time to be realistic, to scale back your aspirations for a world in which justice rolls down like waters and righteousness like a mighty stream, to give up the struggles for others and get what you can for yourself. Well, your challenge for the next half-century is to prove the experts wrong!

BIBLIOGRAPHY

Wright, Conrad, *Beginnings of Unitarianism in America*, Starr King Press, 1955

Wright, Conrad, *American Unitarism* 1805 – 1865, Northeastern University Press, 1989

Owen-Towle, Tom, *The Gospel of Universalism*, Skinner House, 1993

Tiffany, Nina, *Pathbreakers,* Beacon Press 1970

Wright, Conrad, *The Liberal Christians*, Beacon Press, 1970

Scott, Clinton, *These Live Tomorrow*, Beacon Press

Robinson, David, *The Unitarians and The Universalists*, Greenwood Press, 1985

Morrison-Reed, Mark D., *Black Pioneers in a White Denomination*, Skinner House Books, Boston 1980

Tracy, Denise, *A Stream of Living Souls*, Vol. I, II, III

Crompton, Arnold, *Unitarianism on the Pacific Coast,* Beacon Press, 1957

Barton, William R., *The Life of Clara Barton*, AMS Press, New York, 1922

Keller, Gail Faithful, *Jane Addams,* Thomas Crowell Company, New York 1971

Ryan, Cary, *Louisa May Alcott – Her Childhood Library*, Bridge Water Books, 1993

Golemba, Henry, *George Ripley*, Twayne Publishers, G.K. Hall, Boston 1977

Bode, Carl, *Ralph Waldo Emerson – A Profile*, Hill & Wang, New York, 1968

Woodberry, George E., *Ralph Waldo Emerson*, Haskel House, Ltd., New York, 1907

Clifford, Deborah, *Mine Eyes Have Seen The Glory: A Biography of Julia Ward Howe*, Little, Brown & Co.1979

Slater, Abby, *In Search of Margaret Fuller*, Delacorte Press, New York, 1978

Downs, Robert B., *Memorable Americans 1750 – 1950*, Libraries Unlimited, Littleton, CO. 1983

Derleth, August, *Concord Rebel. A Life of Thoreau*, Chilton Company, Philadelphia 1962

Harding, Walter, *Henry David Thoreau – A Profile,* Hill & Wang, New York, 1971

Chevigny, Bell Gail, *The Woman and the Myth – Margaret Fuller's Life and Writings*, Feminist Press, Old Westbury, New York, 1976

Messerli, Jonathan, *Horace Mann, a Biography*, Alfred A Knopf, New York, 1972

Stoddard, Hope, *Famous American Women,* Thomas Crowell Co., New York, 1970

Voss, Carl Herman, *Rabbi and Minister*, World Publishing Co., Cleveland, OH, 1964

Wagenknecht, John Greenleaf Whittier, *A Portrait in Paradox*, Oxford University Press, New York, 1967

Pickard, John B., *John Greenleaf Whittier – An Introduction and Interpretation*, Barnes and Noble, Inc., New York 1967

Mellow, James R., *Nathaniel Hawthorne in His Times*, Houghton Mifflin Company, Boston, 1980

Pringle, Henry, *Life and Times of William Howard Taft*, Farrar & Rinehart, Inc., New York-Toronto 1939

Severn, Bill, *William Howard Taft*, David McKay Company, New York, 1970

Cresson, Margaret French, *Journey Into Fame – The Life of Daniel Chester French*, Harvard University Press, Cambridge, 1947

Richman, Michael, *Daniel Chester French - An American Sculptor*, Metropolitan Museum of Art, New York 1976

Doyle, Edward P., *As We Knew Adlai*, Harper and Rowe, New York, 1966

Brown, Stuart Gary, *Conscience in Politics: Aldai E. Stevenson in the 1950's*, Syracuse University Press, 1961

Martin, John Bartlow, *Adlai Stevenson and the World*, Doubleday & Company Inc. Garden City, New York 1977

Coletta, Poleo E., *The Presidency of William Howard Taft*, University Press of Kansas, 1973

Stone, Irving, *Clarence Darrow for the Defense*, Doubleday & Company, 1941

Weinberg, Arthur & Lily, *Clarence Darrow, A Sentimental Rebel*, G.P. Putnam's Sons, New York, 1980

Wright, Frank Lloyd, *An Autobiography*, Duell, Sloan, and Peace, New York, 1943

Cousins, Norman, *The Healing Heart*, WW. Norton and Company, New York 1983

Cousins, Norman, *Human Options – An Autobiographical Notebook,* WW. Norton and Company, New York 1983

Brabazon, James, *Albert Schweitzer, A Biography*, G.P. Putnam's Sons, New York, 1975

Robles, Harold E., *Albert Schweitzer, An Adventure for Humanity*, the Millbrook Press, Brookfield, Connecticut, 1994

Darwin, Charles, *The Autobiography of Charles Darwin*, W.W. Norton & Company, New York, 1958

Cazden, Elizabeth, *Antoinette Brown Blackwell*, The Feminist Press, Old Westbury, New York, 1983

Fuller, Buckminster, *An Autobiographical Monologue/Scenario*, St. Martin's Press, New York, 1985

Hammond, John Winthrop, *Charles Proteus Steinmetz – A Biography*, D. Appleton-Century Company, New York & London, 1935

Schwartz, Harold, *Samuel Gridley Howe – Social Reformer*, Harvard University Press, Cambridge, 1956

Donald, David, *Charles Sumner and the Coming of the Civil War*, Alfred A. Knopf, New York, 1967

Butterfield, L.H., *The Book of Abigail and John – Selected letters of the Adam's Family*, Harvard University Press, Cambridge and London, 1975

Bober, Natalie S, *Abigail Adams, Witness to a Revolution*, Atheneum Books for Young Readers, Simon & Schuster, New York, 1995

Richards, Laura, *Abigail Adams and Her Times*, D. Appleton and Company, New York, 1920

Whitney, Janet, *Abigail Adams*, Little Brown and Company, Boston, 1947

Binger, Carl, *Revolutionary Doctor – Benjamin Rush*, W.W. Norton & Company, 1996

D'Ella, Donald J., *Benjamin Rush: Philosopher of the American Revolution*, The American Philosophical Society, Philadelphia 1974

AFTERWORD

Good morning. I am
Đon McEvoy

Among the papers my mother left was a notebook of handwritten lectures she had used in teaching an adult class at the First Christian Church in Tulsa, Oklahoma way back in the 1920s and 30s.

Subjects on which she had spoken included:
the sin of racial segregation,
the tragedy and heresy of anti-Semitism,
the need for tolerance of religious cults,
compassion concern for migrant farm workers,
the right of workers to organize and bargain collectively,
the dangers of being led into war by munitions makers,
and opposition to capital punishment.

As I read those manuscripts, which enumerated the very same issues to which I have given my working years, I realized that, apparently, I never had one original idea in my life.

So, why start now? In the proclamation of my Credo I make no claim to originality. Rather, I wish to share some of the lessons I have learned from others with whom I have been privileged to interact across the years, and have sought to incorporate into my own world view. I consider myself extremely blessed those more than three decades of service with the National Conference of Christians and Jews afforded the opportunity for such inspiration.

From Harry Emerson Fosdick I learned a defining principle of making distinctions between right and wrong:
Whatever elevates, enhances and enriches

114

human personality is right.
Whatever diminishes, demeans, or debases
human personality is wrong.
From Rienhold Niebuhr I learned:
"Nothing worth doing can be accomplished in one
lifetime. Therefore, we persevere in hope."
From Martin Luther King, Jr. I learned:
"The measure of a life is not in its duration, but in
its donation." It isn't how long we live, but what
we do with the precious days granted to us.
From Mother Theresa, working with the Peace People in Northern
Ireland:
"Never forget that your most bitter enemy may be God in
clever disguise, testing your ability to forgive."
From Elie Wiesel, survivor and chronicler of the Holocaust, I came
to understand:
"The Bystander, the one who sees injustice and simply
stands aside and does nothing to assist the victim,
is a guilty as the perpetrator of the injustice."
From Adlai Stevenson I learned:
It is better to lose with civility, wit, and integrity intact than
to win by pandering to the dark side of the popular culture.
From Woody Allen:
"I really don't believe in life after death, but I'm
taking along a change of underwear just in case."
From Kermit the Frog – okay, I never really met Kermit, but he
sings my song:
"Someday we'll find it.
The Rainbow Connection,
The lovers, the dreamers, and me."
The Rainbow Connection! That perfect blending of races, colors, cultures and creeds. Someday we'll find it. Not yet. But someday we will. This I believe.

Do not grow weary in well doing or give in to disillusionment and despair. The future belongs to the lovers and dreamers, to you, and to me!